LOS ANGELES

Like a Local

LOS ANGELES
Like a Local

BY THE PEOPLE WHO CALL IT HOME

Contents

meet the locals

SARAH BENNETT
*Sarah's family has lived in the L.A.
area for generations. As an educator
and journalist, Sarah loves sharing
the stories of the land that raised her.
Her mom, a former MGM Studios
executive assistant, would be proud.*

NIGHTLIFE

RYAN GAJEWSKI
*Lifelong L.A. resident Ryan is a staff
editor at The Hollywood Reporter.
When he's not writing, he's sniffing
out banh mi, watching comedy, and
exploring movie studio lots.*

OUTDOORS

ANITA LITTLE
*Writer and editor Anita has been in
L.A. for over a decade, and currently
lives in Culver City with her boyfriend
and cat. She unwinds by wandering
the stacks in indie bookstores and
hiking scenic beach trails.*

EVA RECINOS
*Born and raised in Los Angeles, Eva
is an arts and culture writer. You'll
spot her scribbling away in cafés or
wandering around the city's museums.
She hasn't owned a car in years so,
yes, people do walk in L.A.*

Los Angeles
WELCOME TO THE CITY

Los Angeles – it's all movie star glamour and edgy hip-hop beats, right? Well, yes and no. Much of what you've likely imagined about the city is true: the palm-tree-lined streets, the celebrity sightings, the looming letters of the Hollywood sign. Angelenos really do spend a lot of time outside (who wouldn't when the weather's this good) and the presence of the entertainment industry is basically inescapable. But that doesn't even begin to capture what the real L.A. is like. This isn't just some glossy playground for the rich and famous – it's a sprawling city that millions of ordinary people call home.

And it's those folk who give L.A. its heart. They're a gloriously diverse bunch – around half the population is Hispanic, not that you'd know it from the movies – and they share a sunny outlook that anyone can be anything. They're out-there thinkers launching buzzing pop-ups, fresh-faced hopefuls following

artistic dreams, and immigrants adding new flavors to the epic local food scene. People here don't really sweat the small stuff, though that's not to say that life's always easy. Locals hustle hard to afford the cost of living, and the creep of gentrification is as ever present as the traffic (seriously, whole years are lost stuck in cars). But Angelenos have forged strong communities across the freeways and are fiercely determined to keep L.A. a city for all.

And that's where this book takes you. Beyond the Walk of Fame and into neighborhoods covered with historic street art. To quirky mom-and-pop shops hiding in strip malls and late-night taquerias serving the best birria outside of Mexico. Because that's where the real L.A. lies – in the everyday moments and interactions. So forget everything you've seen on screen, and let us show you the city through the eyes of the locals.

Liked by the locals

"I love that L.A. is so sprawling and diverse that it can't possibly be known in one visit – or even one lifetime. Just when you think you've seen it all, you discover a new pocket to explore, or stumble upon an emerging culture to dive into."

SARAH BENNETT,
FOOD AND CULTURE JOURNALIST

The sun shines on L.A. for around 300 days a year, but the city still has distinct seasons, each with its own traditions and events.

Los Angeles
THROUGH THE YEAR

SPRING

FESTIVAL FUN
Despite a mild winter, Angelenos still celebrate the arrival of spring with a range of festivals across the city. The party continues throughout the season, with St. Patrick's Day in March and Cinco de Mayo in May.

TRAIL TIME
As the days get warmer, L.A.'s super-healthy residents don their best workout gear, lace up their sneakers, and hit the mountain trails to clear the cobwebs.

SHOP 'TIL YOU DROP
The change of season, however minimal, calls for a change of clothes and interior decor. Style mavens head to the likes of the Rose Bowl Flea Market, the Melrose Trading Post, and the Long Beach Antique Market to purge and replenish their wardrobes and homes.

SUMMER

TEAM PLAYER
For many Angelenos, summer revolves around baseball games. Clad head to toe in blue, they flock to Dodger Stadium each weekend to cheer on their team. Go Dodgers!

ALFRESCO MUSIC
Bands and fans move outside to take advantage of the weather at venues like the Greek Theatre, Hollywood Bowl, Levitt Pavilion, and Hollywood Forever Cemetery (yes, you read that right).

PRIDE PARADE

Rainbow flags fly on the second weekend in June, when L.A.'s out-and-proud residents and their allies take to the streets to celebrate the community.

WHERE'S THE SUN?

L.A. doesn't play by the rules and neither does its weather. Summer often sees cloudy, overcast skies, earning the months the nicknames "Gray May," "June Gloom," "No-Sky July," and "Fogust."

FALL

SPOOKY SEASON

The costumes, the makeup, the movies: Hollywood and Halloween have a lot in common. So it's not really surprising that Angelenos throw themselves into the holiday, checking out the theme parks' haunted houses, the Los Angeles Haunted Hayride, and Queen Mary's Dark Harbor.

DÍA DE LOS MUERTOS

On the Day of the Dead, seemingly everyone, from first-generation Mexican immigrants to East Coast transplants, paints their face, dons floral crowns, and parties into the night.

APPLE EVERYTHING

Come fall, locals have one thing on their mind: apples. On the weekends, they drive out to nearby orchards to take advantage of the harvest, sipping fresh cider, and munching on comforting pies. Who said L.A. couldn't be cozy?

WINTER

HOLIDAY CHEER

Okay, you're never going to get a white Christmas in L.A., but in this city you have to fake it till you make it. Locals ice-skate in palm tree-lined Pershing Square and cover their homes in fake snow, bright lights, and blow-up Santas.

NEW YEAR PARADES

It wouldn't be a holiday without a parade. Angelenos ring in the New Year at Pasadena's flower-filled Tournament of Roses Parade and Chinatown's Golden Dragon Parade.

RAINY DAYS

Due to their rarity, a rainy day is a big event in L.A. Expect social media to blow up at the first droplet of water, and the freeways to grind to a complete and utter halt.

There's an art to being an Angeleno, from the do's and don'ts of eating out to negotiating the city's sprawling streets. Here's a breakdown of all you need to know.

Los Angeles
KNOW-HOW

For a directory of health and safety resources, safe spaces, and accessibility information, turn to page 186. For everything else, read on.

EAT
Los Angeles is a city of foodies, so it makes sense that – whatever the hour – there's always some place serving up something truly delicious. Brunch is a huge deal on weekends, with Angelenos waiting in line from 10a.m. for an artful stack of pancakes and a breakfast mimosa. As for dinner, reservations are recommended wherever possible, though some restaurants do have space at the bar for walk-ins.

DRINK
Since L.A. temperatures are pretty mild, the city has plenty of patio cafés and rooftop bars where locals gather for a drink, safe in the knowledge that the sun will (pretty much) always be shining. A beer mostly goes for less than $10, a glass of wine is around $12, and a craft cocktail can cost an eye-watering $20. Thankfully, happy hours are common and make things more affordable. Most bars close around 2a.m.

SHOP
Angelenos love crafting their own unique styles, so it's no surprise they generally prefer to shop at indie boutiques, vintage stores, and flea markets over malls and chain stores. Stores tend to open between 9 and 10a.m., with most closing around 5 or 6p.m. (though malls typically stay open until around 9p.m.). Tip: wherever you're parting with your paycheck, be sure to bring a tote bag. You'll save

yourself a potential charge for a plastic one, and you're doing your part for the environment.

ARTS & CULTURE

Culture usually comes at a price in L.A., with entry to museums and galleries costing anywhere from $9 at smaller venues to $25 for larger institutions. Some also require reservations (even if they are free) so always check ahead. Likewise, it's sensible to book movie tickets before rocking up at the theater.

NIGHTLIFE

Rush hour traffic (think of the opening scene of *La La Land*) makes it pretty difficult to have a spontaneous drink during the week, so Angelenos instead go big on weekends. Predrinking takes place at home or during happy hour. Clubs get going around 10p.m. and generally close at 2a.m. As for what to wear, it depends on the venue: casual clothing is A-OK for a dive bar, while swankier clubs require fancier attire. No matter the place, be sure to carry ID, have a designated driver, and cash for parking.

OUTDOORS

Reading a book on the beach is one of life's simple pleasures, as is chatting with pals over a teetotal picnic (alcohol is prohibited in the city's parks). But there's a lot of dry brush in Los Angeles and wildfires do happen, so be sensible and follow any signs about fire safety. And be sure to take your trash with you – littering carries a fine in California.

Keep in mind

Here are some more tips and tidbits that will help you fit in like a local.

» **Contactless** Most places take cards and methods like Apple Pay, but bring some cash for things like parking.

» **No smoking** Lighting up in public parks, beaches, bus stops, farmers' markets, and outdoor eating areas is banned.

» **Tipping** Adding at least 15, if not 20, percent to your bill is a must at restaurants, bars, and even food trucks.

» **Stay hydrated** Plenty of cafés and restaurants are happy to refill your reusable water bottle – just ask nicely.

GETTING AROUND

Understanding the setup of Los Angeles takes some patience. Sitting within Los Angeles County, with the Pacific Ocean to the west and San Francisco to the north, L.A. comprises various neighborhoods (or communities) and cities (88 of them, to be specific). Chinatown and Bel Air are neighborhoods, for example, while Beverly Hills and Pasadena are technically cities. Angelenos live all over, but most visitors tend to concentrate on the roughly central section between Downtown and Santa Monica. When it comes to navigating the city, locals orient themselves around freeways. The 10 travels east to west, the 110 goes north to south, and the 405 traces the city's western edge.

Once you've got your bearings, L.A. is pretty easy to navigate. But to help you along, we've provided what3words addresses for each sight in this book, meaning you can quickly pinpoint exactly where you're heading.

On foot

It's a myth that locals don't walk in Los Angeles. The city sprawls, yes, and most people own cars (not everyone, mind). But many prefer to enjoy the city's mild climate and palm tree-lined streets by walking. A few words of advice before you set off: distances aren't short (Downtown to Santa Monica is around 15 miles/24 km), and not all neighborhoods are pedestrian friendly (we're looking at you, Bel Air). So you're best off focusing on an area at a time, rather than trying to cover the whole city in one go – Downtown, Santa Monica, the Hollywoods, and Venice are all good places to start. And remember: wear sunscreen, as some blocks don't offer much shade.

On wheels

Biking is not for the faint of heart here in car-happy L.A., but if you're willing to brave it, there are some dedicated bike lanes around the city. Just be sure to put on a helmet before zooming off.

The most relaxed bike paths are on the oceanfront, between Santa Monica and Redondo, and you'll find plenty of bike rentals nearby. If you're exploring more urban areas, Metro Bike Share has docking stations across the city. Just purchase a pass online, download the app, and get pedaling on a classic or electric bike. A 30-minute ride costs $1.75, or you can purchase a $5 one-day pass, which gives you an unlimited number of rides under 30 minutes (though usual charges apply after that). *https://bikeshare.metro.net*

By public transportation

Angelenos like to complain about the Metro, but, in fact, it's a perfectly good way of getting around. Trains run north to south across the city, and also east to west; buses go pretty much everywhere. It's worth buying a $2 TAP card and loading it up with money (it's $1.75 for a one-way fare).

The Los Angeles Department of Transportation's DASH bus service also covers select areas of the city, including downtown L.A., though it doesn't cover as much ground as the Metro.

By car or taxi

Most Angelenos own a car and famously spend a chunk of their lives at the wheel. If you're looking to join them on the road, search for deals on Kayak or Getaround. Use your blinkers and always check your blind spot (though don't assume everyone else will do the same). Parking can be a nightmare so always do your research – including if your destination has a dedicated parking lot, meters, or, well, no parking at all. And be aware that some parking meters take only credit cards or coins.

Prefer to be driven rather than drive? Uber and Lyft are both popular in L.A. though prices can get high, particularly when the city is hosting events.

Download these

We recommend you download these apps to help you get about the city.

WHAT3WORDS

Your geocoding friend

A what3words address is a simple way to communicate any precise location on earth, using just three random words. ///lime.liner.organs, for example, is the code for the entrance to the Griffith Observatory. Simply download the free what3words app, type a what3words address into the search bar, and you'll know exactly where to go.

TRANSIT

Your local transportation service

Map out your journey ahead with Transit, the official Metro app. Not only will it tell you when to transfer to different lines, and which parts of the trip you'll have to walk, but it estimates times when the next bus or train will arrive. No sweat.

L.A. is a sprawling city of cities, and every neighborhood has its own distinct vibe. Here, we take a look at some of our favorites.

Los Angeles
NEIGHBORHOODS

Beverly Hills

90210: it's L.A.'s – heck, the world's – most well-known zip code. And it has all the fancy estates, manicured lawns, and designer boutiques you'd expect from such an iconic haunt of the rich and famous. *{map 3}*

Boyle Heights/East L.A.

This historic area east of Downtown is home to a mostly Mexican community, whose heritage shines through in the robust street food culture and vibrant murals. *{map 1}*

Culver City

The heart of the movie industry in the 1920s, Culver City is now a tech boomtown. It's popular with young professionals, who love its rad mix of dining and culture, and the friendly, small-town feel. *{map 4}*

Downtown

Decades of redevelopment cash have seen the once-seedy Downtown go upscale. These days, there's barely a block without a trendy

new shopping district, art gallery, or restaurant, or a group of revelers hitting up the buzzing nightlife scene. *{map 1}*

Echo Park

Anchored by its namesake park and lake, this gentrified Latinx area is hipster central. In L.A., that means music venues, chic boutiques, and lots of late-night taco trucks. *{map 1}*

Fairfax

When Angelenos don't have weekend plans, they come to this central patch for the Farmers' Market and The Grove. The rest of the time, it's a hub for the city's Jewish community, with delis like Canter's attracting lines throughout the day *{map 3}*

Hollywood

Famed for its unique mix of glitz and grit, plus some pretty iconic landmarks, Hollywood is – of course – the L.A. you know and love from the movies. Expect cinema history and snap-happy tourists aplenty. *{map 3}*

Inglewood

Now home to the biggest and priciest football stadium ever built, not to mention a shiny new NBA arena, this historically Black community is undergoing rapid change as it becomes the latest hub for tourism and sports entertainment. {map 4}

Koreatown

A large Korean population has lived in this neighborhood since the 1960s, though it's been joined in more recent years by other L.A. newcomers. And who can blame them? With cheap rent, convenient shops, and abundant dining, Koreatown has a lot going for it. {map 2}

Little Tokyo

Fun fact: Little Tokyo is one of only three official Japantowns remaining in the U.S. It's a lively hub of Japanese American history and culture, crammed with cool stores and ever-busy food joints. {map 1}

Long Beach

Once the most diverse large city in the U.S., this coastal port is a laid-back mix of urban and suburban. Here, you'll find everyone from college kids to stay-at-home parents to punkers all drinking at the same coffee shops and bars. {map 5}

Los Feliz

With its Old Hollywood bungalows and scenic hillside setting, it's not hard to see why well-heeled creatives are drawn to this artsy enclave. Welcoming, walkable, and packed with trendy cafés and posh galleries, it oozes a vibe that's seriously cool. {map 2}

Pasadena

This has long been the suburb of choice for those wanting to escape the L.A. hubbub and raise a family. Its Old Town gently bustles with parents and retired residents, all browsing the long stretch of chain and independent stores. {map 6}

Santa Monica

This neighborhood may be luxe, but it's never loud about it. Instead, it's a center of easygoing beach vibes, with a daily cast of locals (and a steady stream of tourists) enjoying the sunsets, ocean breezes, and beautiful hikes. {map 4}

Venice

Home to an eclectic mix of tech bros, tourists, and a slowly disappearing immigrant community, this still-funky beach town is famous for its postcard-ready canals and anything-goes boardwalk. Parking is always a battle, but locals love it anyway. {map 4}

West Hollywood

Affectionately known as WeHo to the young creatives who live here, this area has long been the place to come for a good time. Formerly a gambling haven in the 1920s, it's now home to a thumping nightlife scene and a lively LGBTQ+ community. {map 3}

Los Angeles
ON THE MAP

Whether you're looking for your new favorite spot or want to check out what each part of Los Angeles has to offer, our maps – along with handy map references throughout the book – have you covered.

CA-12

CA
SIMI
VALLE

NEWBURY
PARK

OXNARD

US-101

Santa Mon
Mountain

MA

0 kilometers   20

0 miles   20

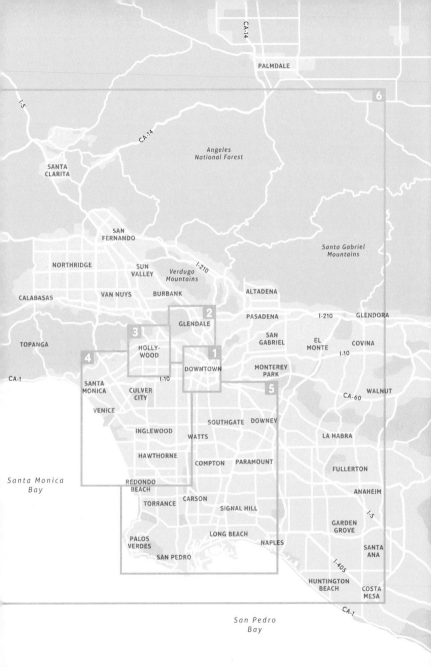

S Cactus Store

ECHO PARK

D Bar Bandini

N The Echo + Echoplex

N Short Stop

N Panamerican Nite Club

O Echo Park Lake

ANGELINO HEIGHTS

HOLLYWOOD FREEWAY

TEMPLE STREET

STREET

SUNSET BOULEVARD

Dodger Stadium

O Elysian Park

ARROYO SECO PARKWAY

A Human Resources

NORTH MAIN ST

D Highland Park Brewing

CHINATOWN

E Howlin' Ray's

Los Angeles River

BEVERLY BOULEVARD

ALVARADO

WESTLAKE

WEST 1ST STREET

WEST 3RD STREET

WILSHIRE BOULEVARD

SOUTH UNION AVENUE

E Philippe The Original

A América Tropical Mural

A El Pueblo de Los Angeles

A Union Station

N Walt Disney Concert Hall

O Grand Park

DOWNTOWN

Grand Central Market

A Los Angeles Central Library

La Cita

N 1st Precinct

S

N **O** Bradbury Building

E The Smell

Fugetsu-Do Confectionery

E Japanese American National Museum

A

LITTLE TOKYO

EAST 1ST ST

A Self-Help Graphics & Art

HARBOR FREEWAY

N Cicada Club

FINANCIAL DISTRICT

SOUTH GRAND AVE

S The Last Bookstore

E Orsa & Winston

EAST 4TH ST

D Death & Co LA

D Arts District Brewing

ARTS DISTRICT

N Exchange LA

N Resident

STREET

SANTA FE AVENUE

E El Parian

D Ace Hotel Rooftop

SOUTH MAIN ST

E Sonoratown

FASHION DISTRICT

STREET

FIGUEROA

SOUTH GRAND AVENUE

EAST MAIN ST

VENICE BOULEVARD

SAN PEDRO STREET

EAST 7TH ST

ALAMEDA STREET

SOUTH

CENTRAL AVENUE

SOUTH

S Bank's Journal

E Bestia

Los Angeles River

WASHINGTON BOULEVARD

SANTA MONICA FREEWAY

0 kilometers | 1

0 miles | 1

MAP 1

LINCOLN
HEIGHTS

1

GOLDEN

STATE

FREEWAY

Re/Arte
Centro Literario
S

A Mariachi
Plaza

BOYLE
HEIGHTS

SANTA ANA

E EAT

Bestia *(p45)*
El Parian *(p41)*
Fugetsu-Do Confectionery *(p49)*
Howlin' Ray's *(p36)*
Orsa & Winston *(p47)*
Philippe The Original *(p37)*
Sonoratown *(p41)*

D DRINK

Ace Hotel Rooftop *(p68)*
Arts District Brewing *(p58)*
Bar Bandini *(p74)*
Death & Co LA *(p67)*
Highland Park Brewing *(p57)*

S SHOP

Bank's Journal *(p83)*
Cactus Store *(p91)*
Grand Central Market *(p101)*
The Last Bookstore *(p96)*
Re/Arte Centro Literario *(p97)*

A ARTS & CULTURE

América Tropical Mural *(p118)*
El Pueblo de Los Angeles *(p110)*
Human Resources *(p131)*

Japanese American National
   Museum *(p109)*
Los Angeles Central Library *(p123)*
Mariachi Plaza *(p109)*
Self-Help Graphics & Art *(p128)*
Union Station *(p121)*

N NIGHTLIFE

Cicada Club *(p136)*
The Echo + Echoplex *(p145)*
Exchange LA *(p154)*
La Cita *(p153)*
Panamerican Nite Club *(p152)*
Precinct *(p150)*
Resident *(p144)*
Short Stop *(p152)*
The Smell *(p146)*
Walt Disney Concert Hall *(p145)*

O OUTDOORS

Bradbury Building *(p177)*
Echo Park Lake *(p168)*
Elysian Park *(p171)*
Grand Park *(p169)*

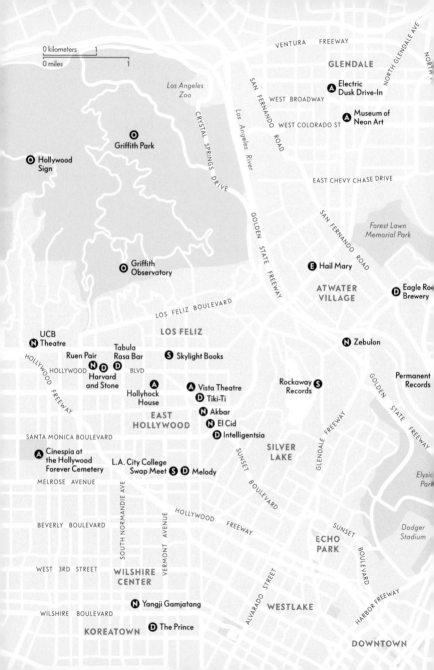

0 kilometers 1
0 miles 1

VENTURA FREEWAY

GLENDALE

Ⓐ Electric
Dusk Drive-In

Ⓐ Museum of
Neon Art

WEST BROADWAY

WEST COLORADO ST

EAST CHEVY CHASE DRIVE

Los Angeles Zoo

CRYSTAL SPRINGS DRIVE

Los Angeles River

SAN FERNANDO ROAD

SAN FERNANDO ROAD

Forest Lawn Memorial Park

Ⓞ Griffith Park

Ⓞ Hollywood Sign

Ⓔ Hail Mary

GOLDEN STATE FREEWAY

ATWATER VILLAGE

Ⓓ Eagle Ro
Brewery

Ⓞ Griffith Observatory

LOS FELIZ BOULEVARD

LOS FELIZ

Ⓝ Zebulon

UCB Ⓝ Theatre

Ruen Pair
Tabula Rasa Bar

Ⓢ Skylight Books

HOLLYWOOD FREEWAY

HOLLYWOOD Ⓝ Ⓓ BLVD
Harvard and Stone

Rockaway Ⓢ Records

Permanent Records

Ⓐ Hollyhock House

Ⓐ Vista Theatre
Ⓓ Tiki-Ti

GOLDEN STATE FREEWAY

EAST HOLLYWOOD

Ⓝ Akbar
Ⓝ El Cid
Ⓓ Intelligentsia

SILVER LAKE

GLENDALE FREEWAY

SANTA MONICA BOULEVARD

Ⓐ Cinespia at the Hollywood Forever Cemetery

L.A. City College Ⓢ Ⓓ Melody
Swap Meet

*Elysia
Par*

MELROSE AVENUE

SUNSET BOULEVARD

SOUTH NORMANDIE AVE

BEVERLY BOULEVARD

HOLLYWOOD FREEWAY

VERMONT AVENUE

SUNSET BOULEVARD

Dodger Stadium

ECHO PARK

WEST 3RD STREET

WILSHIRE CENTER

ALVARADO STREET

HARBOR FREEWAY

Ⓝ Yangji Gamjatang

WESTLAKE

WILSHIRE BOULEVARD

KOREATOWN Ⓓ The Prince

DOWNTOWN

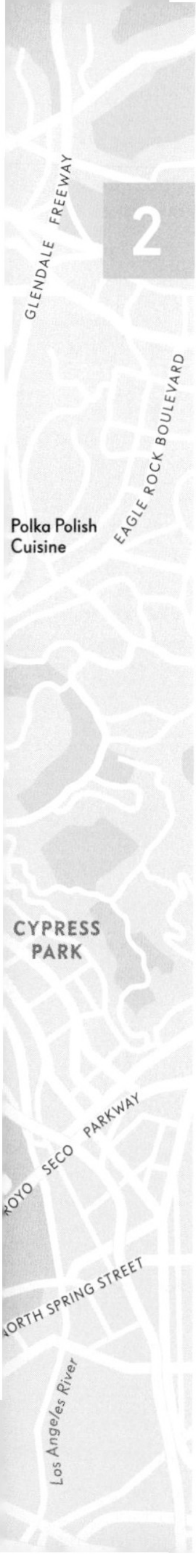

MAP 2

2

GLENDALE FREEWAY

EAGLE ROCK BOULEVARD

Polka Polish Cuisine

CYPRESS PARK

ARROYO SECO PARKWAY

NORTH SPRING STREET

Los Angeles River

🅔 EAT

Hail Mary *(p38)*
Polka Polish Cuisine *(p38)*

🅓 DRINK

Eagle Rock Brewery *(p56)*
Harvard and Stone *(p65)*
Intelligentsia *(p63)*
Melody *(p75)*
The Prince *(p67)*
Tabula Rasa Bar *(p72)*
Tiki-Ti *(p64)*

🅢 SHOP

L.A. City College
   Swap Meet *(p86)*
Permanent Records *(p95)*
Rockaway Records *(p94)*
Skylight Books *(p97)*

🅐 ARTS & CULTURE

Cinespia at the Hollywood
   Forever Cemetery *(p129)*
Electric Dusk Drive-In *(p130)*

Hollyhock House *(p120)*
Museum of Neon Art *(p112)*
Vista Theatre *(p128)*

🅝 NIGHTLIFE

Akbar *(p150)*
El Cid *(p137)*
Ruen Pair *(p158)*
UCB Theatre *(p140)*
Yangji Gamjatang *(p158)*
Zebulon *(p154)*

🅞 OUTDOORS

Griffith Observatory *(p176)*
Griffith Park *(p169)*
Hollywood Sign *(p178)*

MAP 3

BEECHWOOD DRIVE

3

Avalon
Hollywood
Ⓝ
Ⓢ Amoeba
Music
Ⓓ Good Times at
Davey Wayne's

Hollywood
Farmers'
Market

STREET

VINE

MELROSE AVENUE

LARCHMONT

Ⓓ Go Get
Em Tiger

WEST 3RD STREET

WILSHIRE BOULEVARD

Ⓔ EAT

Blu Jam Cafe (p32)
Compartés (p51)
Milk Bar (p49)
Providence (p44)
République (p34)

Ⓓ DRINK

A.O.C. (p75)
E.P. and L.P. (p68)
Go Get Em Tiger (p60)
Good Times at
Davey Wayne's (p65)
The Roger Room (p64)

Ⓢ SHOP

Amoeba Music (p93)
Book Soup (p98)
Decades (p81)
Hollywood Farmers' Market (p102)
The Hundreds (p82)
The Original Farmers'
Market (p102)
The Record Parlour (p92)
Reformation (p82)
RipNDip (p83)
Wild Style LA (p81)

Ⓐ ARTS & CULTURE

Academy Museum (p115)
Craft Contemporary (p113)
Egyptian Theatre (p124)

The Ford (p130)
Los Angeles Contemporary
Exhibitions (LACE) (p133)
New Beverly Cinema (p125)
ONE Gallery (p108)
Schindler House (p122)
Shulamit Nazarian (p130)
Urban Light (p116)
The Wall Project (p117)

Ⓝ NIGHTLIFE

The Abbey (p148)
Avalon Hollywood (p155)
Black Rabbit Rose (p139)
Canter's (p158)
The Comedy Store (p141)
Formosa Cafe (p159)
The Groundlings Theatre (p142)
Hi Tops (p149)
Hollywood Bowl (p146)
Laugh Factory (p142)
The Magic Castle (p137)
Mel's Drive-In (p157)
Pink's Hot Dogs (p157)
The Roxy (p147)
Saddle Ranch Chop House (p139)
Skybar (p154)
Troubadour (p146)

Ⓞ OUTDOORS

Hollywood Walk of Fame (p178)
Mulholland Drive (p180)
Runyon Canyon (p172)

BEVERLY
HILLS

WESTWOOD

E Crustacean

MID-
WILSHIRE

WILSHIRE   BOULEVARD

SUNSET BOULEVARD

SAN VICENTE BOULEVARD

SANTA MONICA BLVD

Attari **E**

BRENTWOOD

Saffron & Rose **E**

WEST SAN VICENTE BLVD

WEST PICO BOULEVARD

Catch One **N**

BEVERLYWOOD

Leo's Tacos **N**   Mateo's **E**

VENICE   BLVD

B Sweet
Dessert Bar **E** **D**   Coffee Tomo **E**

MID CITY

SANTA MONICA FREEWAY

Record Surplus **S**

SAWTELLE

Museum
of Jurassic
Technology

HD Buttercup

Band of Vices **A**

E Bru's
Wiffle

SANTA MONICA FREEWAY

N/naka **E**

A
S **D** Hi-Lo

S Reparation
Club

SANTA
MONICA

E Mélisse

SAN DIEGO FREEWAY

The Ripped
Bodice

Margot

D

O Culver City Stairs

Hot &
Cool Cafe **E**

D Esters Wine Shop & Bar

BUNDY DRIVE

CULVER
CITY

Rolling
Greens

Post & **E**
Beam

S **N** Harvelle's
Santa Monica
Farmers' Market

Art +
A Practic

O
South Beach
Santa Monica

N Circle Bar

MAR
VISTA

S Mar Vista
Farmers' Market

LA CIENEGA BOULEVARD

LA
BREA

AVENUE

HYDE
PARK

CRENSHAW BOULEVARD

VENICE

VENICE   BOULEVARD

E Sunny Blue

High Rooftop **D**

Venice
Beach

MARINA
DEL REY

MARINA FREEWAY

PLAYA
VISTA

Bombay
E Frankie
Company

Foodminati's
The Court Cafe **E**

Hilltop Coffee
+ Kitchen

D

Residency **A**
Art Gallery

VISTA DEL MAR

WEST MANCHESTER AVENUE

INGLEWOOD

WEST

WESTCHESTER

Berbere **S**
Imports

Los Angeles
International
Airport

LENNOX

Dockweiler **O**
State Beach

CENTURY FREEWAY

EL SEGUNDO

HAWTHORNE

El Segundo
Beach

EAST EL SEGUNDO   BOULEVARD

SAN
DIEGO

PRAIRIE AVENUE

CRENSHAW BOULEVARD

Santa
Monica Bay

ROSECRANS   AVENUE

FREEWAY

LAWNDALE

Bruce's Beach **O**

MANHATTAN
BEACH

MANHATTAN   BEACH   BOULEVARD

BEA

REDONDO

0 kilometers   3

0 miles   3

HERMOSA
BEACH   ARTESIA BOULEVARD

LA FRES

Hermosa
City Beach

MAP 4

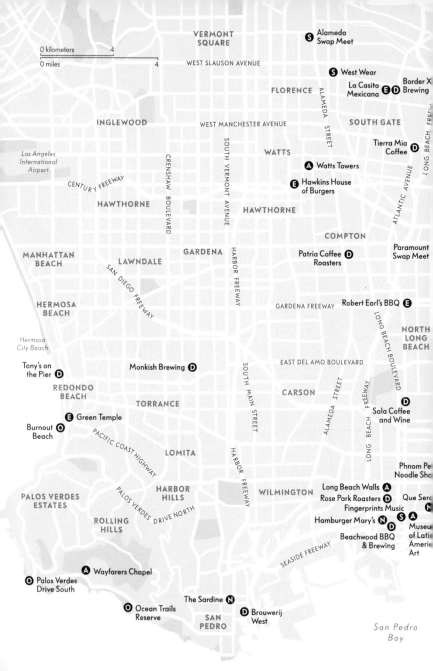

MAP 5

COMMERCE

5

SANTA ANA FREEWAY

PARAMOUNT BOULEVARD

DOWNEY

CENTURY FREEWAY

PARAMOUNT

Ⓔ The Nest

LAKEWOOD BOULEVARD

LAKEWOOD

Ⓢ Long Beach Antique Market

Long Beach Airport

SAN DIEGO FREEWAY

Rancho Los Alamitos Ⓐ

LONG BEACH

Wild Chive

Long Beach Southeast Certified Farmers' Market Ⓢ

Belmont Brewing Company Ⓓ

Ocean Ⓞ Boulevard Ⓢ

Peninsula Bayside Beach Ⓞ

PALMDALE

CA-14

SANTA
CLARITA

I-5

Tía Chucha's Centro Cultural
& Bookstore Ⓢ

SAN
FERNANDO

SIMI
VALLEY

CA-118

Mural Mile Ⓐ

NORTHRIDGE

SUN
VALLEY

Angeles Crest Ⓞ
Highway

I-210

Descanso Ⓞ
Gardens

Mt. Lowe/ Ⓞ
Echo Moun

The Great Wall of
Los Angeles

Circus Ⓞ
Liquor

Flappers Ⓝ

Rose Bowl Flea Mark

Highway 101
30 miles (50 km)
Ⓞ

MacLeod Ale Brewing Company Ⓓ Ⓐ

Ⓔ Porto's Bakery

The Gamble Ho Ⓐ

Ⓢ

Tavern Tomoko &
Ladyface Brewery
Ⓓ

Cici's Cafe Ⓔ

VAN NUYS

BURBANK

Ⓔ

Warner Bros
Studio Tour

Gold Bug Ⓢ Ⓢ Vroman's

PASADENA

Vroman's Ⓞ

Hunting
Library

US-101

Freakbeat Records Ⓢ Ⓓ

Ⓢ

Smoke
House

Leaf and Ⓢ
Spine

Ⓓ Blind
Barber

Augustine
Wine Bar

Studio
City
Farmers'
Market

Ernest E. Ⓞ
Debs Park

Ⓔ Bánh Mì
My-Tho

Santa Monica
Mountains

TOPANGA

Murphy
Ranch Ⓞ

I-405

DOWNTOWN

Ⓐ Vincent Price
Art Museum

Leo Carrillo State Park
7 miles (11 km)
Ⓞ

Los Liones Ⓞ

MALIBU

I-10

Ⓞ

Solstice
Canyon

Ⓞ Ⓞ

Zuma Ⓞ Ⓞ
Beach Point
Dume

Pacific Coast
Highway Ⓞ

SANTA
MONICA

CULVER
CITY

VENICE

INGLEWOOD

See maps 1–5
for Central Los Angeles

SOUTHGATE

DOWNEY

I-5

Santa Monica
Bay

I-105

WATTS

HAWTHORNE

COMPTON

Santa Fe Springs
Swap Meet

REDONDO
BEACH

I-405

CARSON

SIGNAL HILL

TORRANCE

PALOS
VERDES

LONG BEACH

NAPLES

SAN PEDRO

San Pedro
Bay

0 kilometers   10

0 miles   10

MAP 6

6

Bridge to Nowhere
10 miles (16 km)
O

Chantry
Flat   Joshua Tree
            National Park
210   125 miles (200 km)
                      O
Chatterbox
Comedy **N**
TE   COVINA
    I-10

A The Donut
    Hole

CA-60   **O**
ns to Pines Scenic Byway
95 miles (155 km)

LA HABRA

FULLERTON
        CA-91
I-5   ANAHEIM

    The Frida **A**
CA-22 Cinema

            SANTA
            ANA
I-405

TINGTON
EACH
        COSTA
        MESA

E EAT

Bánh Mì My-Tho *(p40)*
Cici's Cafe *(p33)*
Porto's Bakery *(p51)*
Smoke House *(p46)*

D DRINK

Augustine Wine Bar *(p72)*
Blind Barber *(p67)*
MacLeod Ale Brewing Company *(p58)*
Tavern Tomoko & Ladyface Brewery *(p70)*

S SHOP

Gold Bug *(p90)*
Freakbeat Records *(p93)*
Leaf and Spine *(p90)*
Rose Bowl Flea Market *(p85)*
Santa Fe Springs Swap Meet *(p84)*
Studio City Farmers' Market *(p102)*
Tia Chucha's Central Cultural & Bookstore *(p99)*
Vroman's *(p98)*

A ARTS & CULTURE

The Donut Hole *(p122)*
The Frida Cinema *(p130)*
The Gamble House *(p123)*
The Great Wall of Los Angeles *(p117)*
Mural Mile *(p118)*
Vincent Price Art Museum *(p115)*

N NIGHTLIFE

Chatterbox Comedy *(p142)*
Flappers *(p141)*

O OUTDOORS

Angeles Crest Highway *(p182)*
Bridge to Nowhere *(p175)*
Chantry Flat *(p172)*
Circus Liquor *(p176)*
Descanso Gardens *(p171)*
Ernest E. Debs Park *(p168)*
Highway 101 *(p182)*
Huntington Library *(p171)*
Joshua Tree National Park *(p183)*
Leo Carrillo State Park *(p166)*
Los Liones *(p174)*
Mt. Lowe/Echo Mountain *(p174)*
Murphy Ranch *(p173)*
Pacific Coast Highway *(p181)*
Palms to Pines Scenic Byway *(p182)*
Point Dume *(p177)*
Solstice Canyon *(p175)*
Warner Bros Studio Tour *(p179)*
Zuma Beach *(p166)*

EAT

Slurp Cambodian soup for breakfast, snack on Mexican tacos for lunch, and savor Korean BBQ for dinner – L.A. offers endless culinary delights, bursting with global flavors.

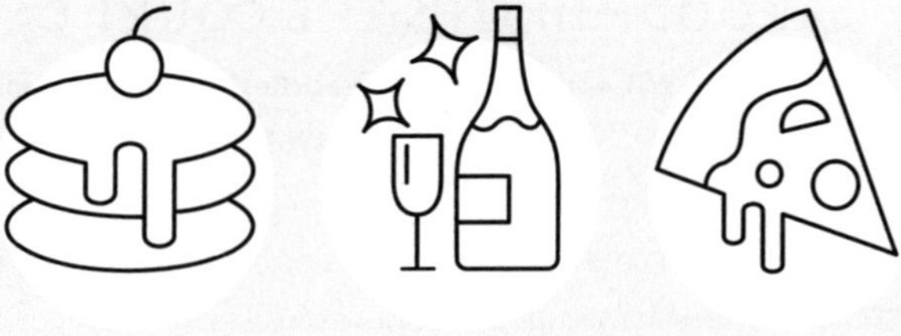

Brunch Spots

In Los Angeles, brunch is celebrated like a religion, with top destinations filling up faster than a Sunday service. It's a ritual faithfully observed by all – obligatory glass of mimosa firmly in hand.

BLU JAM CAFE

Map 3; 7371 Melrose Avenue, West Hollywood; ///steps.packet.final; www.blujamcafe.com

For a classic L.A. brunch experience, look no further than Blu Jam. Here, hearty portions of organic Benedicts, overstuffed omelets, and Mexican staples like chilaquiles are served alongside a carefully curated selection of coffees. There are now seven locations around the city (always packed with a crowd), but the Melrose Avenue original is still our favorite for a weekend group hang.

FOODMINATI'S THE COURT CAFE

Map 4; 5496 W. Centinela Avenue, Westchester; ///mice.complains.rally; (310) 431-4969

What more fitting headquarters for a (not-so-) secret food society than a low-key café in a nondescript strip mall? Founded by a pair of chefs with cult followings on social media, it's a chamber of culinary

Check out The Court Cafe's Instagram feed to discover why the chefs have a devoted social media following.

wonders – think lobster and waffles, taco omelets, and decadent French toast sandwiches. What better way to start a lazy Sunday?

GREEN TEMPLE

Map 5; 1700 S. Catalina Avenue, Redondo Beach; ///tins.rope.cage; www.greentemple.net

Any thoughts of traffic-filled freeways are soon banished at this beachside vegetarian haven. Its leafy patio is the hideaway of health-conscious South Bay locals, who catch up over the soothing soundtrack of a burbling koi-filled fountain. Dishes on the eclectic menu range from walnut loaf to Asian-influenced veggie bowls, all washed down with a mandatory glass of frothy green juice. It's enough to get anyone a bit closer to finding inner peace.

CICI'S CAFE

Map 6; 18912 Ventura Boulevard, Tarzana; ///books.drips.claps; www.ciciscafe.com

Drawing hordes of hungry patrons from across the San Fernando Valley, the menu at Cici's will satisfy even the most demanding sweet tooth. There are 80 (yes, 80) different pancake varieties, nearly all of which come topped with whipped cream. For first-timers, the green tea tiramisu or chocolate velvet options are safe and scrumptious bets.

» Don't leave without trying the pillowy soufflé pancakes. Trust us, they're a decadent treat to die for.

WILD CHIVE

Map 5; 2650 E. Broadway, Long Beach; ///riches.dazzling.same;
www.thewildchive.com

After years of serving her mouthwatering vegan brunches through pop-ups, chef Soozee Nguyen finally landed her own brick-and-mortar establishment. Great news for Long Beach regulars (and visitors), who can now wolf down her meat-free Monte Cristos, mushroom burgers, and breakfast banh mi whenever they want.

RÉPUBLIQUE

Map 3; 624 S. La Brea Avenue, Hancock Park; ///bats.freed.froth;
www.republiquela.com

Husband-and-wife chef team Walter and Margarita Manzke run a veritable food empire, including buzzy Filipino counter Sari Sari Store and upscale Parisian bistro La Bicyclette. But République is where it all started. While the dinner menu here gets the most hype, weekend brunch is where it really shines brightest: Walter's French-influenced dishes sing harmoniously with Margarita's fresh breads and pastries.

Try it!
PICNIC BRUNCH

The Saturday farmers' market in downtown Santa Monica offers an incredible selection of flaky organic pastries. Grab a mix of sweet and savory treats and wander down to the beach for a picnic brunch.

BRU'S WIFFLE

Map 4; 2408 Wilshire Boulevard, Santa Monica; ///puzzle.spite.occurs;
(310) 453-2787

Everyone from movie execs to college students battles for tables at this Westside chicken-and-waffle joint. Of course, the go-to is anything involving fried chicken and a waffle – like the huevos rancheros, which also includes eggs, guacamole, beans, and cheese. Because, why not?

THE NEST

Map 5; 9260 Alondra Boulevard, Bellflower; ///limes.issue.learn;
www.eatnest.com

It's fair to say the remote suburb of Bellflower is not one of L.A.'s top foodie hot spots. Thanks to this friendly Latinx breakfast joint, however, that's set to change. Making its name are standout dishes like the churro waffle and the breakfast poutine – oh, and the iced coffees are a caffeine addict's dream.

PHNOM PENH NOODLE SHACK

Map 5; 1644 Cherry Avenue, Long Beach; ///menu.fight.included;
www.thenoodleshack.com

Fun fact: Long Beach is reportedly home to the largest population of Cambodians outside Southeast Asia. And where better to start exploring the community's heritage than this quick-fire Cambodian soup joint. Noodles for breakfast? Yes, please.

» Don't leave without ordering *kuyteav*, a traditional Cambodian breakfast soup served with a pork bone broth.

Comfort Food

Like much else in L.A.'s culture, what qualifies as comfort food breaks all the rules. Instead of hearty soups and stews, Angelenos find cheer in a mix of nostalgic standbys that soothe the soul.

HOWLIN' RAY'S

Map 1; 727 N. Broadway #128, Chinatown; ///punt.glee.smashes; www.howlinrays.com

Inspired by the punchy heat of Nashville's famous hot chicken, this cramped counter in Chinatown's foodie Far East Plaza was the pioneer behind L.A.'s Southern sandwich craze. The lines are forever long (no less than an hour, be prepared for up to five) and the fried chicken almost sparkles with fiery red spice, but you'll undoubtedly find yourself desperate for more.

HAWKINS HOUSE OF BURGERS

Map 5; 11603 Slater Street, Watts; ///dream.palm.wants; www.hawkinsburgers.com

You'd think the monstrous burgers at Hawkins were invented to be Instagrammed, but it was back in 1939 that James Henry Hawkins started slinging his signature patties. Each burger is built on a foundation of craggy, half-pound Angus, pristinely charred at the edges and densely wrapped in toppings as tame as tomato and lettuce and as intense as hot links, pastrami, and eggs. Served from a building smooshed against the 105 Freeway, they're a favorite with neighbors from the public housing projects across the street.

ROBERT EARL'S BBQ
Map 5; 703 Artesia Boulevard, Long Beach; ///form.serve.snipe; www.robertearlsbbq.com

For most of his adult life, Robert Earl was a backyard pit master, serving slow-smoked Texas-style dishes at family gatherings and catering gigs alongside the day job. In 2012, he started rolling his smoker over to his hometown farmers' market and – one award-winning brick-and-mortar roadhouse later – the rest is L.A. BBQ history.

PHILIPPE THE ORIGINAL
Map 1; 1001 N. Alameda Street, Downtown; ///voters.pinks.souk; www.philippes.com

The fight over who invented the French dip is as old and heated as L.A. itself. Look, every version of this jus-dipped roast beef sandwich is delicious, but when it comes to an experience that's as comforting as the food, Philippe's is the clear winner. Since 1908, lunch here has been an L.A. rite of passage for everyone, from downtown construction workers to fresh-faced arrivals from nearby Union Station.

» **Don't leave without** ordering a second sandwich. The roast beef is legendary, but there's also lamb, turkey, pastrami, pork, and ham.

LA CASITA MEXICANA
Map 5; 4030 E. Gage Avenue, Bell; ///oddly.crowned.mixed;
www.casitamex.com

It's hard to imagine a Mexican food scene in L.A. without Jaime Martin del Campo and Ramiro Arvizu, the celebrity chef duo who opened La Casita Mexicana in 1999. This place is truly iconic, serving regional specialties with immense love and pride.

» Don't leave without ordering the *chile en nogada* (chilies in walnut sauce), a classic dish that incorporates the colors of the Mexican flag.

HAIL MARY
Map 2; 3219 Glendale Boulevard, Atwater; ///saying.turns.silent;
www.hailmarypizzala.com

Forget the pies of New York and Chicago. L.A.'s pizza scene has grown out of the city's artisanal bakeries, and you can taste the difference in the dough. Hail Mary is a great place to try this new crust culture, with its signature sourdough base and seasonal toppings.

POLKA POLISH CUISINE
Map 2; 4112 Verdugo Road, Glassel Park; ///stands.purely.cafe;
www.polkarestaurant.com

Don't have a Polish grandmother to make you piping hot pierogi? Homey Polka has you covered. Founded by two Polish expats with a heart for their homeland's cuisine, this modest strip mall joint is a mainstay for nostalgic Eastern Europeans and young Eastsiders looking for a hug on a plate.

Liked by the locals

"I wanted to make a crust
and pizza that I wanted to eat.
Naturally leavened sourdough,
whole grains, and organic and
locally grown ingredients. Nothing
fussy, just a commitment
to quality."

DAVID WILCOX,
HAIL MARY OWNER

Quick Bites

As laid-back as L.A. is, spending your life stuck in traffic can leave little time for sustenance. Luckily, there are lots of places with rapid-fire service that can whip up a great meal in minutes.

SUNNY BLUE

Map 4; 12608 W. Washington Boulevard, Culver City;
///spice.fend.grass; www.sunnyblueinc.com

If you want quick but also delish, you can't beat the highly snackable *omusubi* (Japanese rice balls) at this small Culver City counter. On any weekday afternoon you'll find studio workers stocking up on the handcrafted morsels, stuffed with crowd-pleasing fillings like kara tuna, miso beef, and sautéed eggplant with chili miso. Can't decide? Nothing on the menu is more than $5, so just get one of everything.

BÁNH MÌ MY-THO

Map 6; 304 W. Valley Boulevard, Rosemead; ///rounds.punk.sulk;
www.banhmimytho.com

Admittedly, this San Gabriel gem isn't the top choice if you're in a genuine hurry – it's a bit of a drive and you'll likely have to wait in the inevitable line – but its Vietnamese banh mi are so good you'll

Remember to hit up the ATM on your way to Bánh Mì My-Tho; the small shop is cash only.

wolf them down in seconds. Think generously sized portions of flavorful meat or tofu, drizzled with spicy aioli and tightly wrapped inside a cloud-soft bun.

EL PARIAN

Map 1; 1528 W. Pico Boulevard, Downtown; ///gender.causes.shell; (213) 386-7361

Birria (stewed goat) tacos are having an indisputable moment in the L.A. food scene, with more and more trucks serving up the fat-dipped Jaliscan specialty. But this family-owned institution is no trend hopper. They're veterans in the game, preparing birria for loyal regulars and in-the-know enthusiasts for nearly 50 years. It's the real deal, right down to the ranchera music trickling out of the jukebox.

SONORATOWN

Map 1; 208 E. 8th Street, Downtown; ///lend.thinks.dairy; www.sonoratown.com

When restaurateurs Teodoro Diaz-Rodriguez Jr. and Jennifer Feltham opened this joint, the pair had one mission: to serve traditional north Mexican tacos, stuffed with perfectly prepared carne asada. It's safe to say they nailed it – this restaurant is regularly packed with downtown office dwellers and Latinx neighbors scarfing down fat burritos and tangy salsa roja.

» Don't leave without buying a bag of homemade flour tortillas – they're some of the best in the city and sold to-go if you ask.

Solo, Pair, Crowd

Spend any time in L.A. and you'll soon notice its plentiful taco trucks – handily, that means there's an option for every occasion.

FLYING SOLO
Eat on the fly
Ricky's Fish Tacos, with its mean crispy fish with smoky, spicy red salsa, makes a great grab-and-go lunch for one. Check Twitter to find out where the truck will be each day.

IN A PAIR
Lunchtime date
Mariscos Jalisco is very no frills and that's the way we like it, thank you very much. This lunch truck (there are five around the city) is great for a budget-friendly day date. Order a selection of ceviche tostadas to share.

FOR A CROWD
Feast with friends
If you like dipping delicious things into other delicious things, then Teddy's Red Tacos is for you. Bring some friends and feast on *birria* consomé tacos at one of the city's 10 Teddy's trucks.

ATTARI

**Map 4; 1388 Westwood Boulevard, Little Tehran;
///learns.analogy.crowd; www.atarisandwiches.info**

Tucked away off the trafficky Westwood Boulevard, this sandwich shop is one of Little Tehran's best-kept secrets. You won't find classic cold cuts here – instead, the Persian expats and occasional UCLA students lunching in its tree-lined courtyard come for the tongue and brain sandwich (trust us), finished off with a bite of baklava.

CHICHÉN ITZA

**Map 4; 3655 S. Grand Avenue c6, Downtown; ///album.robots.king;
www.chichenitzarestaurant.com**

Chef Gilberto Cetina opened this joint in 2001, and since then has enjoyed nonstop acclaim for his Yucatán-inspired fare. The humble counter serves up amazing *cochinita pibil* (slow-roasted pork tacos) that will linger in your mind long after your lunch is over.

BOMBAY FRANKIE COMPANY

**Map 4; 6000 Sepulveda Boulevard Suite 1601, Culver City;
///indeed.flood.liked; www.thebombayfrankiecompany.com**

The brainchild of an Indian American brother-sister duo raised in L.A., this Indian burrito spot started life as a side offering at a gas station. Now in a stand-alone space in the Westfield Mall, it's still attracting a devoted following with its tasty modern street food.

» Don't leave without trying the crowd-pleasing chicken tikka masala Frankie (Indian burrito), wrapped in tandoor-baked garlic naan.

Special Occasion

L.A. may not be inundated with Michelin stars, but that doesn't mean the city lacks in fine dining. These celebration-worthy spots focus on chef-driven food, elevating the eating experience beyond the everyday.

PROVIDENCE

Map 3; 5955 Melrose Avenue, Hollywood; ///spices.hobby.skill; www.providencela.com

Just because you have a Michelin star or two, doesn't mean you have to be showy. For almost 20 years, this Hollywood hideaway has been quietly luring well-heeled regulars with the simple promise of the city's finest sustainable seafood. Yes, you might have to forgo this month's rent money to eat here, but the epic eight-course tasting menu is totally worth it.

N/NAKA

Map 4; 3455 Overland Avenue, Palms; ///slime.margin.fall; www.n-naka.com

Okay, you'll need perseverance and/or luck to get a table here (there are only 26 seats and reservations disappear in seconds), but hang on in there until you do. Chef Nikki Naka's California take on Japanese *kaiseki* – a traditional dinner of small plates, featuring locally grown, seasonal ingredients – is an utterly exquisite experience. If you're tempted to rejoin the reservation queue, do – she famously never serves guests the same dish twice.

MÉLISSE

Map 4; 1104 Wilshire Boulevard, Santa Monica; ///trial.anyway.pools; www.citrinandmelisse.com

Snobby scenesters might see this restaurant's white tablecloths and formal decor as stuffy, but Mélisse clearly isn't concerned about keeping up with design trends. And why would it, when dishes like clam chowder custard and coffee-crusted lamb have won it two Michelin stars? The intimate setting makes this a great place to celebrate an anniversary (just book in advance).

BESTIA

Map 1; 2121 E. 7th Place, Arts District; ///exact.sticks.format; www.bestiala.com

The 2012 launch of this too-cool Italian restaurant single-handedly revived the Arts District food scene – and it's been a battle to snag a table here ever since. Thankfully, despite its reputation, the swanky joint still manages to feel approachable and inviting, its industrial-chic dining room humming with the chatter of lucky local creatives as they catch up over plates of the city's best pasta.

» **Don't leave without** trying something from the impressive wine list – all bottles are biodynamic.

POST & BEAM

Map 4; 3767 Santa Rosalia Drive, Leimert Park; ///food.equal.full;
www.postandbeamla.com

As you step onto the verdant patio of Post & Beam, the twinkly porch
lights, fragrant herb garden, and live R&B music immediately make
you forget you're in a city. And the homey atmosphere only gets cozier
as you tuck into the elevated Southern cooking. Traditional soul
food like shrimp and grits or honey cornbread is front and center
here, as part of a menu celebrating Black heritage.

SMOKE HOUSE

Map 6; 4420 Lakeside Drive, Burbank; ///pouch.listed.email;
www.smokehouse1946.com

Since opening its doors down the street from the Warner Bros.
studio in 1946, this hangout has remained an industry favorite. The
dark, cozy atmosphere has ensnared legions of famous fans, from
Hollywood heavyweights of yore like Judy Garland and James Dean

Shh!

Run by the owners of Post &
Beam, Black Pot Supper Club
(www.postandbeamla.com/
hemings-hercules) is South L.A.'s
only outdoor dinner series
celebrating historic African
American cuisine. Snag a
reservation at one of these
intimate events to experience
a new take on Black cooking.

to contemporary heartthrobs like George Clooney (who named his production company after it). Settle into the classic red leather booths and savor solid steakhouse staples like prime rib and lobster tail.

» **Don't leave without** ordering the famous garlic cheese bread. As all regulars know, it's not a visit to the Smoke House without it.

ORSA & WINSTON
Map 1; 122 W. 4th Street, Downtown; ///modern.grows.desk; www.orsaandwinston.com

Although Orsa & Winston is on the splurge-y end of chef Josef Centeno's downtown foodie empire (he's up to four restaurants so far), you can still treat yourself without breaking the bank. For $125, you'll receive a five-course tasting menu inspired by Italian and Japanese flavors – though it's usually closer to 10, with all the in-between amuse-bouches that float out from the kitchen.

CRUSTACEAN
Map 4; 468 N. Bedford Drive, Beverly Hills; ///salsa.crash.fleet; www.crustaceanbh.com

After fleeing Saigon in 1971, the An family went on to pioneer the modern Vietnamese food movement in San Francisco, before bringing their talents to Beverly Hills. Their much-loved L.A. institution has long sat at the top of the seafood scene, with the roasted king crab and garlic noodles becoming legends in their own right. It's a fave with Hollywood A-listers and the Beverly Hills elite, as proven by the not-so-subtle paparazzi milling about outside.

Sweet Treats

*Pastry chefs and ice-cream shops and sugary drinks,
oh my! L.A. is a hotbed of sweets and desserts, thanks
to a creative fusion of immigrant traditions and
dishes designed for drool-worthy social media posts.*

MATEO'S

**Map 4; 4234 Pico Boulevard, Mid City; ///sticks.finest.thus;
www.mateosicecreamla.com**

Usually, the best Mexican ice-cream stores in L.A. have "Michoacana"
in the name, a nod to the Mexican state famed for its traditional
creamy desserts. But this mini chain of strip mall shops is the exception
that proves the rule. Our favorite location is the first-ever store in
Mid City, where local families are lured by dozens of tempting flavors,
piles of fresh fruits, and a rainbow of *paletas* (Mexican popsicles).

B SWEET DESSERT BAR

**Map 4; 2005 Sawtelle Boulevard, Sawtelle; ///liked.analogy.hotels;
www.mybsweet.com**

Ever since her humble food truck beginnings, self-taught chef
Barb Batiste has been at the forefront of L.A.'s Filipino food movement. Inspired by her mother's home cooking (from the heart, no

Cans of B Sweet's signature cold brew coffee and sugar-free teas are sold in many health food stores. measurements, lots of purple yam), she doles out her famous bread puddings, seasonal cheesecakes, and still-moist cookies in portions built to share.

FUGETSU-DO CONFECTIONERY

Map 1; 315 E. 1st Street, Little Tokyo; ///also.shell.gains; www.fugetsu-do.com

Specializing in the taffy-like mochi, this Japanese confectionery has been a mainstay of Little Tokyo for more than a hundred years. Its third-generation owner, Brian Kito, is a master mochi craftsman who uses a mix of rice, gelatin, and flour to execute impossible feats of color, texture, and flavor. Each piece is a delicate masterpiece that's almost too good-looking to eat (but no, really, you should eat it).

» Don't leave without trying both classic mochi, filled with bean paste, and *ogura*, which flips the mochi inside out with a bean paste exterior.

MILK BAR

**Map 3; 7150 Melrose Avenue, Fairfax; ///flames.envy.intro;
www.milkbarstore.com**

Don't be put off by the perpetual line: the goodies inside Milk Bar's West Coast flagship are as sweet as its pink decor. And the line is all part of the fun, anyway. Not only do you get to peek inside the bakery's combination classroom, commissary, and R&D lab, but you get plenty of time to ogle the small but formidable menu of addictive shakes, cakes, and truffles. The hardest part of the whole experience is narrowing down what to order.

Solo, Pair, Crowd

**I scream, you scream, we all scream
for somewhere to eat ice cream –
thankfully, L.A. has plenty of options.**

FLYING SOLO
Filipino quick fix

Satisfy that sweet tooth at one of L.A.'s few
Jollibees (a Filipino fast-food chain). Go for
the halo-halo, a decadent dessert layered
with beans, ice, and condensed milk – it's just
as good as Jollibee's famous Yumburger.

IN A PAIR
A taste of Italy

Impress your date by transporting them to
a classic Italian gelateria – without ever
leaving the Valley. It's here that the famous
Italian chain Fatamorgana Gelato opened
its first location outside of Rome, serving
nearly 70 flavors daily.

FOR A CROWD
Korean classic

Korean shaved ice, aka *bingsoo*, is not
designed to be eaten alone. Gather the
crew and head to Sul & Beans, where even
a small size of this loaded-up dessert
will feed a whole party.

PORTO'S BAKERY

Map 1; 3614 W. Magnolia Boulevard, Burbank; ///resort.study.grapes;
www.portosbakery.com

A trip to this family-run Cuban bakery (or one of its four sister branches) is like participating in a carefully choreographed ballet. Unending lines of families wait their turn to pick from the glossy cakes and tropical tarts, while dozens of workers dance behind a gleaming counter in an organized chaos that must be seen to be believed.

SAFFRON & ROSE

Map 4; 1387 Westwood Boulevard, Little Tehran; ///broker.spike.blend;
www.saffronrosepersianicecream.com

A meeting place for Persian expats, UCLA students, and young Westside families, this ice-cream parlor is the unofficial city hall of Little Tehran. Scoops come in Middle Eastern flavors like pistachio, orange blossom, and, of course, the store's namesake saffron and rose.
» Don't leave without trying a scoop of *faloodeh*, a rosewater-flavored sorbet marbled with rice noodles.

COMPARTÉS

Map 3; 516 N. La Brea Avenue, Hancock Park; ///boost.camera.grab;
www.compartes.com

Always dreamed of visiting Willy Wonka's chocolate factory? Here's the next best thing. Compartés' gourmet chocolate bars — flecked with everything from sea salt to potato chips — have been luring customers with childlike delight since as far back as the 1950s.

A foodie afternoon in
Koreatown

The 1960s saw record numbers of Koreans move to the West Coast. One such person was Hi Duk Lee, a businessman with a vision. The grocery store owner set out to remedy L.A.'s lack of businesses serving immigrants like him, by buying a block of streets to house Korean-owned stores and restaurants. Today, this patch remains a hub for the community, as well as a hot spot for Korean fare. Spend some hours eating your way around this mini city, which locals say rivals the streets of Seoul.

1. Surawon Tofu House
2833 W. Olympic Boulevard;
(213) 383-7317
///yoga.sadly.fund

2. SomiSomi
621 S. Western Avenue
#208-A; www.somisomi.com
///relax.wiping.feared

3. Cafe Mak
612 Shatto Place;
(213) 252-9898
///hails.flock.fats

4. Quarters Korean BBQ
3465 W. 6th Street #C-130;
www.quarterskbbq.com
///pads.spicy.eggs

WEST   3RD

Sate your sweet tooth at
SOMISOMI

Indulge in a customized
ah-boong, a fish-shaped waffle
cone stuffed with soft-serve
ice cream and your choice of
colorful toppings (think rainbow
sprinkles and mini macarons).

WEST   OLYMP

WEST   PICO

📍 **Olympic Boulevard and Normandie Avenue**
///fried.rips.factories

SOUTH NORMANDIE AVENUE

SOUTH VERMONT AVENUE

VIRGIL AVENUE

WEST 3RD STREET

REET

Line up at
QUARTERS KOREAN BBQ

Wait it out for a table at this beloved Korean BBQ restaurant, where guests cook their chosen meats on the tableside grill and gorge on an endless stream of *banchan* (assorted pickled snacks).

WILSHIRE CENTER

4

Linger at
CAFE MAK

This tea and coffee shop serves cups of caffeine a dozen ways. Our top pick? It's between the plum tea and Korean-style coffee.

WEST 6TH STREET

WEST 6TH STREET

3

WILSHIRE BOULEVARD

WILSHIRE BOULEVARD

HOOVER STREET

SOUTH VERMONT AVENUE

IROLO STREET

WEST 8TH STREET

WEST 8TH STREET

KOREATOWN

STREET

1

Start at
SURAWON TOFU HOUSE

Fuel up for the afternoon ahead by tucking into a gurgling pot of *soondubu jjigae*, a spicy soup made with house-made tofu.

Hi Duk Lee purchased streets around **Olympic Boulevard** *and* **Normandie Avenue** *as a starting point for Koreatown.*

WEST OLYMPIC BOULEVARD

WEST PICO BOULEVARD

SOUTH VERMONT AVENUE

PICO UNION

| 0 meters | 500 |
| 0 yards | 500 |

DRINK

With its classically Californian good weather, L.A. was made for relaxing outdoors with a drink. Sip wine on a sunny patio, drink beer by the beach, or swig coffee in leafy courtyards.

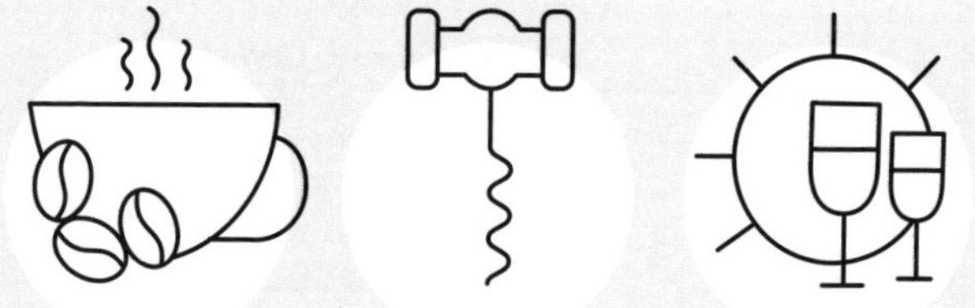

Breweries

For a long time San Diego ruled the SoCal beer scene, but now L.A. is challenging for the crown. With boundary-pushing breweries in every corner of the county, you're never far from a good pint.

EAGLE ROCK BREWERY

Map 2; 3056 Roswell Street Suite A, Glassell Park; ///click.than.event; www.eaglerockbrewery.com

Looking to chill after a busy week? This family-run brewery is the perfect place to unwind. Serving American takes on classic European beer styles, its homey tasting room is a favorite of beer nerds and local parents, who are often found playing board games over a pint. Order a glass of the Populist American IPA and just kick back.

Try it!
BREW YOUR OWN

Inspired by L.A.'s homebrewers-turned-pros? You can buy raw materials for making your own beer at the Home Beer Wine Cheesemaking Shop in Woodland Hills *(www.homebeerwinecheese.com)*.

MONKISH BREWING

Map 5; 20311 S. Western Avenue, Torrance; ///hugs.define.blocks; www.monkishbrewing.com

If you're the kind of person who tracks hype in the craft beer world, Monkish needs no introduction. After launching the brand in 2012 with a focus on Belgian-style beers, brewmaster Henry Nguyen decided to test his talents as a yeast whisperer on an emerging style: the New England IPA. Less like traditional bitter IPAs and closer in flavor to juicy oatmeal pale ales, Monkish's hazy IPAs have become legendary outside L.A. They still have a strong local fan base, mind you, as attested by the beach bums and beer industry workers you'll find in the brewery's taproom.

HIGHLAND PARK BREWING

Map 1; 1220 N. Spring Street, Chinatown; ///pencil.thanks.verse; https://hpb.la

It's not only in Hollywood where you'll find a great rags-to-riches story. Highland Park's tale begins in the early days of L.A.'s beer scene, when a humble homebrewer set up shop in the tiny back rooms of a former escort club. With little more than a bathroom drain and space to make only a few kegs at a time, Bob Kunz started creating crisp, sessionable ales and lagers as house brewer for The Hermosillo bar. Cut to now, and he's the proud owner of this dedicated downtown tasting room, where the hoppy pilsners and zippy IPAs are the delight of local hipsters.

» Don't leave without trying Hello L.A., Highland Park Brewery's first IPA and a classic balanced-but-bold Los Angeles take on the style.

ARTS DISTRICT BREWING

Map 1; 828 Traction Avenue, Arts District; ///employ.raced.civic;
www.artsdistrictbrewing.com

When Arts District Brewing opened at the end of 2015, L.A.
had never seen a tasting room quite like it. Built into a multilevel
converted ice house, it features an arcade's worth of Skee-Ball
machines and a 100-ft- (30-m-) long central wood bar (with an
impressive selection of top-shelf liquor). The beers are as majestic
as the cavernous space – hit up your friends and get a crowd
together so you can make a proper night of it.

BROUWERIJ WEST

Map 5; 110 E. 22nd Street, Warehouse No. 9, San Pedro;
///genre.unguided.pavers; www.brouwerijwest.com

With its waterfront warehouse setting and annual summer music
festival, Brouwerij West positively oozes coastal California cool.
And it's not just us who think that – young drinkers flock here from
the entire South Bay area, drawn by the funky beers sold in must-
collect cans, all designed by local artists.

MACLEOD ALE BREWING COMPANY

Map 6; 14741 Calvert Street, Van Nuys; ///spend.curl.meant;
www.macleodale.com

Is that the roil of bagpipes in the distance? Don't worry; you're not
imagining things. The owners of MacLeod Ale Brewing Company
are members of L.A.'s small but mighty community of Scots and

For a true British pint, order one of the cask ales – they're served in traditional British 20 oz glasses.

started brewing as a way to fund their bagpipe troupe's competitions. Happily for everyone, the beer piped from the kegs is just as melodious as the tunes.

BEACHWOOD BBQ & BREWING
Map 5; 210 E. 3rd Street, Long Beach; ///upcoming.sublime.whips; www.beachwoodbbq.com

For the majority of its existence, Beachwood BBQ & Brewing's beers have swept every major competition in which they were entered. (Oh, and it was officially named one of the world's best brewpubs at the World Beer Cup in 2016.) But you wouldn't guess it. This low-key spot is reliably laid-back, with a mix of regulars quietly sipping on brash IPAs and savoring pan-American BBQ by the cozy firepit.
» Don't leave without trying the winelike beers from Beachwood Blendery, the Belgian sour ale project around the corner.

BORDER X BREWING
Map 5; 4400 E. Gage Avenue, Bell; ///walks.sunk.cycle; www.borderxbrewing.com

After earning a reputation for its beers inspired by Mexican cuisine, this San Diego brand expanded its reach with a huge brewery, tasting room, and event space in Bell. It's become a popular meeting place for the neighborhood's young Latinx community, who catch up over beers celebrating their heritage. Think saisons spiked with ruby-red hibiscus and golden stouts that taste like cinnamon rice milk.

Coffee Shops

As every Angeleno knows, caffeine is the key to creativity (and, well, happiness in general). From funky college coffee shops to third-wave minimalist joints, here are the best places in the city to find a cup of joe.

COFFEE TOMO

Map 4; 11309 Mississippi Avenue, Sawtelle; ///healthier.bench.lied; (310) 444-9390

Are you at Coffee Tomo for the hand-dripped cup of single-origin joe or the giant artisanal pretzel filled with sweet potatoes and mozzarella? We say come for both. Everything at this gourmet coffee shop is crafted to perfection, from the work-of-art lattes to the calming Japanese design aesthetic.

GO GET EM TIGER

Map3; 230 N. Larchmont Boulevard, Larchmont; ///stove.gear.shovels; www.gget.com

Coffee is more than just a drink in L.A.: it's a way of life. And nowhere is that more true than Go Get Em Tiger (or GGET). Set up by two champion baristas, this rapidly expanding L.A. chain has essentially become its own lifestyle brand. Its hip neighborhood cafés serve

carefully curated beans and restaurant-quality food, with a line
of branded clothing on the side. Our favorite branch is this one in
Larchmont, where the long counter creates a cool, barlike vibe.

» **Don't leave without** eating something. Each location has its own
menu; here, it's all about breakfast goodies like pastries and waffles.

PATRIA COFFEE ROASTERS

Map 5; 108 Alameda Street, Compton; ///courier.manage.audit;
www.patriacoffee.com

One of the few independently owned coffee shops amid the sprawling
grid of South Los Angeles, Patria is a co-op roastery and retail space
that serves its community while supporting it, too. Events like bike
rides and film screenings are held here on weekends, but most days
you'll find young creatives tapping away on MacBooks, reading the
local literary journal (shout out to *Dryland*), and sipping house-
roasted beans from across Latin America.

HOT AND COOL CAFE

Map 4; 4331 Degnan Boulevard, Leimert Park; ///beyond.wipes.groups;
www.hotandcoolcafe.com

They say that a coffee shop can be the heart of a community,
and Hot & Cool Cafe is living proof of that. Since opening on a
cozy retail strip in the heart of historic Black L.A., the vegan social
enterprise and roastery has become the neighborhood's artistic and
cultural hub. Sip a seasonal cold brew while attending anything
from a concert to a sermon to a political meeting.

TIERRA MIA COFFEE

Map 5; 4914 Firestone Boulevard, South Gate; ///jump.decide.alarm;
www.tierramiacoffee.com

Who says great coffee has to mean high-concept spaces and prices? Not Tierra Mia. This locally spawned chain is a breath of fresh air, with a proudly Latin vibe that honors the heritage of its beans. Each branch nestles into a historic Latinx neighborhood, repurposing whatever architecture defined the location before (in El Monte, an A-frame Mexican fast-food walk-up; in Long Beach, a former Taco Bell). Shops also have no Wi-Fi, so instead of laptop-bound drones, you'll find conversations — between *abuelas* and grandkids, friends and business associates, and servers and regulars.

» Don't leave without trying Tierra Mia's famous horchata or dulce de leche lattes. They can also be ice blended for a cold buzz on warm days.

ROSE PARK ROASTERS

Map 5; 800 Pine Avenue, Long Beach; ///howler.marked.bolts;
www.roseparkroasters.com

The philosophy at Rose Park is simple: the best cup of coffee is the one you make at home. The team will even deliver the beans to your door by bicycle, so if you wanted, you could get your daily caffeine fix without ever leaving the house. But that would be a mistake. Without coming in-store, you'd miss specials like the maple lavender latte, or the mint agave matcha tea. And you'd also miss out on the amazing food. The menu here is the experimental wonderland of Michelin-trained chef, army vet, and general

On weekends, Ortiz often partners with other local chefs for one-off collaborative "Family Meals."

Long Beach legend Melissa Ortiz. Her creative brunches and seasonal seafood dinners are totally worth getting dressed for, trust us.

HILLTOP COFFEE + KITCHEN
Map 4; 170 N. La Brea Avenue, Inglewood; ///cabin.speak.froze; www.findyourhilltop.com

South of the 10 Freeway, there aren't a lot of inspiring spaces where people can get creative over a quality brew. That's where Hilltop Coffee + Kitchen comes in. Its first store was such a hit with actress Issa Rae that she partnered with the owners to bring this second location to her hometown of Inglewood. Who knows – as you sip locally sourced coffee and munch on a gourmet breakfast, maybe you'll rub shoulders with the creator of the next *Insecure*.

INTELLIGENTSIA
Map 2; 3922 Sunset Boulevard, Silver Lake; ///safely.winter.wrong; www.intelligentsia.com

In 2007, when Intelligentsia opened this glass-and-steel Silver Lake flagship, specialty coffee culture was way outside L.A.'s comfort zone. The Chicago-based brand essentially launched the city's third-wave coffee scene, and now it's hard to imagine a time when single-origin hand pours weren't standard. If all the hipsters and Eastside creatives here are anything to go by, it looks like Intelligentsia's premium craft coffee will be around a while yet.

Cocktail Joints

L.A.'s cocktail scene has always mixed up its own flavors. Sure, you can still find the classics, but how about a nouveau Tiki drink or a seasonal cocktail featuring shrubs from the bartender's backyard?

TIKI-TI

Map 2; 4427 W. Sunset Boulevard, Los Feliz; ///input.monkey.served; www.tiki-ti.com

After years mixing drinks at Hollywood's legendary Polynesian-themed bar Don the Beachcomber, Ray Buhen founded his own spot, Tiki-Ti, in 1961. The crowded dive, now owned by Ray's son and grandson, draws a young, hip crowd for a drink menu that's changed little since its early days. House favorites include Ray's Mistake, which dates back to 1968 and features passion fruit and a dark rum float.

THE ROGER ROOM

Map 3; 370 N. La Cienega Boulevard, Beverly Grove; ///visit.today.toned; www.therogerroom.com

Of course one of L.A.'s finest cocktail bars is right next to the Largo comedy theater – this is the home of show business, after all. Though don't come here expecting any glitz and glamour. The mood at the

Roger Room is more dive-bar chic, with dark lighting and cozy booths. The drinks served here pack a suitably powerful punch – Death in the Afternoon (with absinthe and prosecco) anyone?

HARVARD AND STONE
Map 2; 5221 Hollywood Boulevard, Thai Town; ///deals.frozen.spin; www.harvardandstone.com

A World War II theme is perhaps not what you might expect for this bar's Thai Town location. But, somehow, the vintage-industrial vibe feels just right for the grungy-but-cool East Hollywood neighborhood. Expect live rock music, top-tier mixology, and the occasional burlesque performance thrown in for good measure.

» Don't leave without checking out the backroom bar, which is often taken over by guest bartenders with seasonal cocktail menus.

GOOD TIMES AT DAVEY WAYNE'S
Map 3; 1611 N. El Centro Avenue, Hollywood; ///saving.sock.gazed; https://goodtimesatdaveywaynes.com

Bored of generic nights out? So are the Houston brothers. They're shaking up L.A. with their epic speakeasies and have truly outdone themselves with Davey Wayne's (named after their dad). Step inside a replica of the family garage, open the refrigerator door, and enter a retro haven full of laid-back 1970s charm. Lounge chairs overflow with cool 20-somethings, while friendly mixologists whip up tasty concoctions like the Fat Elvis (peanut-infused rye whiskey, blackberry shrub, and creme de cacao). Dad would approve.

Solo, Pair, Crowd

Speakeasies are an obvious fit for a city famed for its storytelling – no wonder L.A. is full of them.

FLYING SOLO
Silent cinema
An easy-to-miss red door in an unremarkable alleyway leads to, well, The Red Door, a mellow San Fernando Valley gem. Don't worry about not having anyone to chat to – you can sip a drink while watching silent movies on the TVs.

IN A PAIR
Eighties vibes
The Slipper Clutch sets an upbeat mood with its 1980s-inspired setting and colorful lights. It's a fun spot for catching up with a pal – and enjoying a bit of friendly competition on the pinball machines.

FOR A CROWD
Drink and a dance
Part speakeasy, part club, Lock & Key is a great place to bring the whole gang. Everyone will appreciate the care taken by the bar staff, who prepare drinks with freshly squeezed juices and house-made syrups.

THE PRINCE

Map 2; 3198 1/2 W. 7th Street, Koreatown; ///steps.dock.filled; (213) 389-1586

Ever wished your life was more like a sitcom? Grab a drink at
the bar where Nick Miller (Jake Johnson) worked in *New Girl*.
Part restaurant, part bar, this neighborhood fave is as loved for
its Korean fried chicken as it is for its craft cocktails.

BLIND BARBER

**Map 6; 5715 N. Figueroa Street, Highland Park; ///guess.finishing.spaces;
https://blindbarber.com**

Unlike most of the city's speakeasies, the facade at Blind Barber is
actually a functioning business – if you arrive before 8p.m., you can
sit down for a trim. In the evenings, it's all about the hidden bar out
back, where dates meet for an intimate after-work sip.

» Don't leave without trying a delicious Hot Heather, featuring
tequila, grapefruit, pineapple, lime, and ginger.

DEATH & CO LA

**Map 1; 818 E. 3rd Street, Arts District; ///worth.music.brain;
www.deathandcompany.com**

Pull up a barstool for a lesson in expert mixology – this West Coast
outpost of the famed New York City bar can offer you a cocktail for
every mood. Bad audition? Drown your sorrows with a rum-heavy
Banned in D.C. Closed a major deal? Celebrate with a whisky-based
Queen of the Rodeo. Using local, seasonal ingredients, the bartenders
take the art of cocktail making to a whole new level.

Terraces and Rooftops

You didn't come to L.A. to drink inside. Sit at any of these expansive outdoor dining areas, your favorite cocktail in hand, and take in the city's year-round sunshine and stellar views.

ACE HOTEL ROOFTOP

Map 1; 929 S. Broadway, Downtown; ///pirate.young.scuba; www.acehotel.com

Ace is the epitome of downtown rooftop cool – with its industrial charm, great live music, and super-chill clientele – but thankfully without the pretension (no boat shoes or polos here). Come with a pal and kick back over a perfectly made Manhattan.

E.P. AND L.P.

Map 3; 603 N. La Cienega Boulevard, West Hollywood; ///gave.crest.mops; www.eplosangeles.com

Looking for a stereotypical social media-ready rooftop scene? This West Hollywood bar and restaurant overdelivers, with its nighttime views of the Hollywood Hills that are good enough to rival a postcard. On the buzzing deck you'll find L.A. rich kids glowering into their specialty cocktails, friends out celebrating birthdays, and stylistas who just want someone to notice their designer sneakers. The only drawback is the difficulty of getting in – there's always a line out the door on weekend nights.

TONY'S ON THE PIER

Map 5; 210 Fisherman's Wharf, Redondo Beach; ///marker.dinner.softly; www.oldtonys.com

Since the 1950s, "Old Tony's" has been offering no-nonsense locals affordable mai tais and panoramic views of the water right on Fisherman's Wharf. The old-school seaside vibe – complete with fishing nets hanging from the ceiling – is perfectly complemented by its charming pier location and classic seafood dishes. (The oysters are some of the freshest you'll find in the South Bay.)

» **Don't leave without** ordering a mai tai. It's so legendary that it even comes in a souvenir glass you get to take home.

HIGH ROOFTOP

Map 4; 1697 Pacific Avenue, Venice; ///glow.flames.cheat; www.hotelerwin.com

Sitting atop the trendy Hotel Erwin, this lively cocktail bar is a great spot to see all of L.A. life on the Venice boardwalk below. Don't be put off by the intimidating bouncers – you'll find everyone feels at home here, whether that's nervous first dates, overdressed tourists, or surfer bros coming in from the waves.

BELMONT BREWING COMPANY

Map 5; 25 39th Place, Long Beach; ///wiser.cheater.dices;
www.belmontbrewing.com

Right on the water, this brewpub – the oldest one operating in
SoCal – attracts both sun-weathered old-timers and fresh-faced
students with pitchers of classic brews. Enjoy miles of oceanfront
and city skyline while sipping on award-winning ales.

» Don't leave without trying the Long Beach Crude – an easy-drinking
stout brewed in honor of the nearby Signal Hill oil field.

TAVERN TOMOKO & LADYFACE BREWERY

Map 6; 29281 Agoura Road, Agoura Hills; ///cracker.pixies.pushed;
www.taverntomoko.com

Looking out from this bar's veranda, with its hilly views of Ladyface
Mountain, you could almost imagine you're in the south of France.
That's what owner Cyrena Nouzille thinks, anyway, and she does her
best to complete the fantasy with her wonderful French-style brews.

MARGOT

Map 4; 8820 Washington Boulevard, Suite 301, Culver City;
///blur.grin.lazy; www.margot.la

The crown jewel of the Culver City restaurant revival, this airy rooftop
joint has people from both sides of the 10 Freeway scrambling for
a reservation. Join the lucky few sipping regional wines and craft
cocktails while taking in 360-degree views of the city.

Liked by the locals

"The rooftop bar craze may have kicked off in N.Y.C., but L.A. perfected it. I can't really think of a better city where you can knock back a pisco sour after work while looking down at the ocean waves almost any time of the year."

ANDREA LEE, SOCIAL MEDIA MANAGER
AND SKINCARE INFLUENCER

Wine Bars

With California's wine country just up the coast, it's no surprise that L.A. is full of cozy wine bars. Whether they're championing rare vintages or eco-friendly newbies, staff will gladly guide you to your perfect sip.

AUGUSTINE WINE BAR

Map 6; 13456 Ventura Boulevard, Sherman Oaks; ///strong.single.basket; www.augustinewinebar.com

Not everyone has the bank balance of the movie stars who live in the Hollywood Hills, so if you want to taste a rare vintage wine without spending a fortune, this is the place to go. Pick a year and let the bartender pour you a glass.

TABULA RASA BAR

Map 2; 5125 Hollywood Boulevard, Thai Town; ///among.coins.glue; www.tabularasabar.com

A Thai Town hangout with an excellent selection of natural wines, Tabula Rasa is one of the best wine bars on this side of the city – though it's so laid-back, you wouldn't know it. The vibe here is ultra-chilled, with a low-key industrial aesthetic, mellow mood lighting, and the easy beats of old-school hip-hop in the

Go during the late afternoon happy hour (4–6p.m.) when it's just $2 a glass for all wines.

background. If you've had a total nightmare of a day stuck in traffic, there's no better place to come and unwind.

SALA COFFEE AND WINE

Map 5; 3853 Atlantic Avenue, Long Beach; ///with.wisdom.grills; (562) 269-0476

Coffee and wine: two beverages dear to the heart of many an Angeleno. And Sala does both exceptionally. Call by in the morning for a caffeinated pick-me-up, then return in the afternoon to lazily linger over a bottle of red. The welcoming staff are always open to questions – they love to rave about their wine picks as much as the young, largely Latinx clientele loves to drink them.

» **Don't leave without** ordering a light bite from whichever friend of the owner's is taking over the kitchen that day.

HI-LO

Map 4; 8582 Washington Boulevard, Culver City; ///paths.lifted.remote; www.hiloliquor.com

More than your friendly neighborhood liquor store, this spot has a special, boutique feel. Part wine shop, part tasting room, it offers hard-to-find wine and beer, charming staff who know the liquor industry from top to bottom, and a gorgeous, well-curated space (plus fun bodega snacks like popped water lily seeds). The best part? As the name suggests, you'll find great pours whatever your budget.

BAR BANDINI

Map 1; 2150 W. Sunset Boulevard, Echo Park; ///rungs.page.linen;
www.barbandini.com

Don't let Echo Park's hipsters know we've told you about Bar
Bandini – they want to keep this local gem all to themselves. And
who can blame them? Chic but relaxed, it's an intimate place that's
just as good for trying to impress a date as it is for a hangout with
your best friends. The rotating selection of wines is perfectly on
trend (read: natural and organic), and if you ask politely they'll
even let you sample a few before pouring a glass. Oh, and they
also have a pretty good beer selection, too.

ESTERS WINE SHOP & BAR

Map 4; 1314 7th Street, Santa Monica; ///rainy.spice.epic;
www.esterswineshop.com

Tucked away from Santa Monica's main street in an elegantly restored
Art Deco building, this upscale space – with its cushy lounge seating
and see-and-be-seen patio – is the domain of the neighborhood's

Try it!
TRAIN YOUR TASTE BUDS

Learn the art of being a sommelier with
Sunday tastings at Esters Wine Shop &
Bar. You'll get a themed tasting from the
250-plus selection, curated by in-house
expert Randall Elliot.

rich and fashionable. Yes, it's spendy, but who doesn't enjoy a bit of glamour every once in a while? Treat yourself: order a full bottle and some plates of charcuterie (we highly recommend the smoky dates and lavender almonds).

A.O.C.

Map 3; 8700 W. 3rd Street, West Hollywood; ///strike.patch.salt; www.aocwinebar.com

Walking into this warmly lit restaurant and bar, with ivy crawling up the tiled walls, you might think you've left L.A. and arrived at a lush Spanish villa. Founded by a SoCal sommelier duo, this West 3rd Street location has an iconic wine list that pairs beautifully with its Mediterranean-style small plates. If you're on a date, be sure to ask for seating on the romantic, fairy-tale patio.

» **Don't leave without** ordering the Spanish fried chicken – it makes a great accompaniment to a bottle of chardonnay.

MELODY

Map 2; 751 N. Virgil Avenue, East Hollywood; ///quiz.papers.urban; www.melodyla.com

With a bright turquoise front and electric-blue neon trim, this energetic neighborhood wine joint is difficult to miss. Inside, you'll find lively groups of friends drinking generous pours and snacking on creative food from rotating pop-ups. The overall feel is like being at a dinner party, where the drinks and conversation flow so easily you don't realize you've been sitting there for hours.

An evening of cocktails in
classic Hollywood

Ah, Hollywood, the birthplace of the movie business. Back in the golden age of cinema, in the 1930s, Tinseltown was dominated by five movie studios and produced 600 films every year. By the middle of the century, however, low theater admissions and censorship rulings meant the industry dwindled, with all but one studio closing. The neighborhood was revitalized in the 80s and regained its popularity – this time for nightlife. A place where tumbledown dives sit next to sexy speakeasies, Hollywood is known for its blend of glamour and grit. So make like you're a star of the silver screen and swig a cocktail in style.

1. Frolic Room
6245 Hollywood Blvd;
(323) 462-5890
///event.trail.excuse

2. Musso and Frank
6667 Hollywood Blvd;
www.mussoandfrank.com
///breath.energy.actor

3. No Vacancy
1727 N. Hudson Ave;
www.novacancyla.com
///cuts.valley.images

4. The Spare Room
7000 Hollywood Blvd; www.
spareroomhollywood.com
///critic.woes.depend

 Dolby Theatre® ///feeds.bounty.deal

HOLLYWO
HEIGHT

FRANKLIN AVEN

Have a ball at
THE SPARE ROOM
End the night with a game of bowling at this cocktail lounge inside the Hollywood Roosevelt Hotel. It was cofounded in 1927 by then-MGM honcho Louis B. Mayer and silent film stars Mary Pickford and Douglas Fairbanks.

HOLLYWOOD
DELL

NORTH
CAHUENGA
HOLLYWOOD
FREEWAY
BLVD

AVENUE
HIGHLAND

FRANKLIN
AVENUE

*The **Dolby Theatre®***
has hosted the annual
Academy Awards
ceremony since opening
in 2001, when the 74th
Awards were presented.

Imbibe and pretend at
NO VACANCY

This perennial hot spot doesn't actually
date back to Hollywood's golden age.
You wouldn't know it, though, thanks to
actors helping set the vintage scene as
you enjoy period-appropriate cocktails.

3

LLYWOOD   BOULEVARD   2   HOLLYWOOD   BOULEVARD   1

HOLLYWOOD

Turn back the clock at
MUSSO AND FRANK

Hollywood's oldest restaurant, which
first opened in 1919, has always had a
never-ending list of famous fans, from
Marilyn Monroe to Harrison Ford.
Ask for one of the famous martinis.

Dive in at
FROLIC ROOM

Next door to the historic Pantages Theatre,
this low-key bar started life as a speakeasy
in 1930 before attracting the likes of Judy
Garland and Frank Sinatra. Order a cheap
drink, sit back, and enjoy people-watching.

ST   SUNSET   BOULEVARD   WEST   SUNSET   BOULEVARD

AVENUE

HIGHLAND

STREET

VINE

OUNTAIN   AVENUE   FOUNTAIN   AVENUE

SHOP

The L.A. look is a perfectly styled blend of modern design and one-off vintage finds. From clothes to books to produce, it's all about keeping it cool and local.

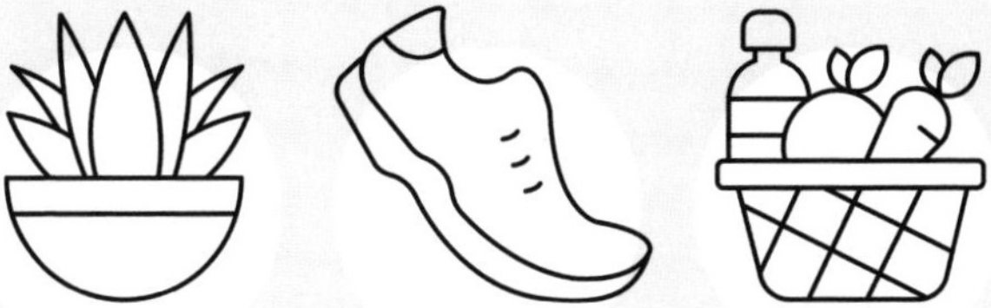

Street Style

One of the world's newer fashion headquarters, L.A. is home to an effortlessly cool street style that's still accessible to all. Think casual but high-end: a pair of fresh sneakers, comfy jeans, and your smartest tee.

WEST WEAR

Map 5; 6207 Pacific Boulevard, Huntington Park; ///feels.thank.costs; www.westwear.com

L.A. wasn't always a hard-core sports town, but ever since the Dodgers (baseball), Lakers (basketball), and Rams (football) became national champions, Angelenos are required to rep gear supporting at least one of the three. Pick your favorite and make your way to unassuming West Wear, where sports fans shop for budget-friendly deals. It's got

Try it!
GO TO A GAME

Now you've got the gear from West Wear, why not show it off at an actual game? Catch a fixture at Dodgers Stadium, watch the Lakers at the Crypto.com Arena, or cheer on the Rams at the SoFi Stadium.

a floor-to-ceiling selection of sports and lifestyle apparel, ready to supply you with all of the hats, socks, and jerseys you could ever possibly want. Go team!

WILD STYLE LA

Map 3; 7703 Melrose Avenue, Melrose; ///thick.crate.brand; https://wildstylela.com

Want to know what the next big trend will be? Head over to Wild Style. Founded by Tim Hirota, the creative genius behind premium streetwear label Joyrich, the sprawling store showcases the future of street fashion, one up-and-coming designer at a time. It's a favorite with the rich and famous, who are as desperate as anyone else here to be ahead of the curve.

» **Don't leave without** walking across the street to the Joyrich boutique to see what kind of "wearable art" is being sold this season.

DECADES

Map 3; 8214 Melrose Avenue, Melrose; ///crash.corner.tiles; https://decadesinc.com

There are plenty of places in L.A. to buy vintage fashion, but there's only one Cameron Silver and only one Decades. Known as the "Duke of Melrose," Silver trawls through estate sales (and the closets of celebrities and socialites) before selling his finds at this perfectly curated consignment store. His knack for amassing one-of-a-kind pieces is the envy of the city's wardrobe stylists and deal-hunting fashionistas, who pilgrimage here for secondhand designer gems.

REFORMATION

Map 3; 8000 Melrose Avenue, Beverly Grove; ///shades.quench.sage; www.thereformation.com

If you don't think eco-friendly womenswear can be sexy, then you've never seen someone in a Reformation dress. The cute, sustainable pieces fall somewhere between the fast fashion of Zara and the haute couture of Rodeo Drive, attracting cult followers in droves. Check out the Ref vintage store down the road, too.

THE HUNDREDS

Map 3; 501 N. Fairfax Avenue, Fairfax; ///spare.major.form; www.thehundreds.com

The staff here may have a reputation for high snobbery, but that doesn't deter all the skaters, hip-hop heads, and cool kids found browsing in the showroom. The Hundreds is, after all, one of L.A.'s

Yes, you can order clothes from Galerie.L.A. online *(www. galerie.la)* , but it's much more fun to make an appointment and shop in real life at the Long Beach showroom. That way, you can talk to Dechel Mckillian, the company's enthusiastic founder and eco-brand evangelist (she's also a celebrity stylist). Her aim is to curate items that match her customers' values, so you'll find garments arranged by categories like BIPOC-owned, ethical production, and vegan.

most iconic streetwear brands, its graphic tees becoming something of a local uniform. Look carefully and you'll spy its exploding cartoon "Adam Bomb" logo all over town.

» **Don't leave without** admiring the giant mastodon skeleton sculpture breaking through the shop's floor.

BANK'S JOURNAL

Map 1; 1320 E. 7th St, Downtown; ///class.gladiators.them; www.banksjournal.com

In L.A., nothing says modern coastal style quite like breezy organic cotton tees and recycled-bottle swim trunks. (All made ethically in your favorite muted color, of course.) And nowhere sells any that are quite as good as those at Bank's Journal. The brand's airy boutique exudes all the ease of a casual summer day, with oodles of tapered twill pants and vintage-style shirts to browse, too.

RIPNDIP

Map 3; 441 Fairfax Avenue, Fairfax; ///proof.smashes.leader; www.ripndip.com

Who, we hear you ask, is that mischievous kitty you keep seeing around? You know, the one peeking out of a T-shirt pocket or painted on a wall – with the *Mona Lisa* smile and middle finger crudely raised? This, friends, is Lord Nermal: the viral star of RipNDip. A tongue-in-cheek brand born out of skate culture, RipNDip sells tees, hoodies, and skateboard decks from this gleaming white-walled flagship. It's a super-cool space that's as edgy as his lordship.

Swap Meets and Flea Markets

Malls, schmalls. The real retail heart of Los Angeles is its swap meets and flea markets, where vendors set up rows of stalls and shoppers descend to buy, well, anything and everything.

ALAMEDA SWAP MEET

Map 5; 4501 S. Alameda Street, Central-Alameda; ///cable.rice.noise

Make sure you're wearing comfy shoes – exploring the Alameda Swap Meet is a full-day affair. Spread over several city blocks, this huge indoor bazaar offers every item and service imaginable. Where else can you buy a birthday gift, stock up on cleaning supplies, enjoy a foot massage, grab a taco, and get your taxes done in one go?

SANTA FE SPRINGS SWAP MEET

Map 6; 13963 Alondra Boulevard, Santa Fe Springs;
///opinion.energetic.cars; http://sfsswapmeet.com

"Come for the bargains … stay for the fun." So says the Santa Fe Springs slogan, and we couldn't have put it much better ourselves. Part marketplace, part concert venue, it's got the lively buzz of a town square. Families browse for discount car parts and children's toys, while a youthful crowd make a beeline for the food and entertainment (weekends feature an eclectic mix of cover bands and Latin sounds). It's not often you'll find a swap meet open for afternoon and evening shopping, so make the most of it.

LONG BEACH ANTIQUE MARKET

Map 5; 4901 E. Conant Street, Long Beach; ///decreased.expect.scouted; www.longbeachantiquemarket.com

Looking to accessorize your place with a super-stylish vintage coffee-table book? Or how about an exquisitely restored Eames chair? Perhaps an old tin sign, too? You'll find all these and more at Long Beach Antique Market, a veritable homewares heaven. Held on the third Sunday of every month, it offers style from the past at bargain prices.

» **Don't leave without** buying something decorative for the house – an old freeway sign, say, or a set of 1950s shot glasses.

ROSE BOWL FLEA MARKET

Map 6; 1000 Rose Bowl Drive, Pasadena; ///fully.fancy.ships; www.rgcshows.com/rose-bowl

The $12 admission to this monthly "Flea Market of the Stars" might seem steep, but can you really put a price on easy access to 2,500 of the country's top pop-up vintage and thrift stores? We don't think so. And neither do the Silver Lake hipsters and industry designers who flock here monthly, all desperate to find their next treasure.

L.A. CITY COLLEGE SWAP MEET

Map 2; 4133 Marathon Street, East Hollywood;
///weedy.battle.looked; http://laccswap.com

Okay, to be fair, the "LACC Swap" is more like a large weekend garage sale than a true swap meet (where you'd find a labyrinth of market stalls). But for only $1 admission, you can join East Hollywood's rapidly changing Central American community as they scour the stalls for clothing, housewares, and even produce. If you can't decide whether to splash out on that vintage Dodgers tee, just remember that one-third of the meet's sales revenue goes toward scholarships at L.A. City College – so you're not just treating yourself; you're giving back to the neighborhood, too.

PARAMOUNT SWAP MEET

Map 5; 7900 All America City Way, Paramount; ///song.agents.lift;
www.paramountswap.com

Breaking up the South L.A. sprawl, Paramount is a daily swap meet with acres upon acres of rock-bottom-priced goods. Why, yes, that is an entire table of untouched insulated tumblers for $3 each. And did you see the rows of discount gold and silver jewelry? What about all the tag-on lingerie and socks being sold for pennies on the dollar? Even if you're not running low on homewares and undergarments, the deals here are too good to resist. Show up with a $20 bill and go home happy.

» Don't leave without getting a *michelada* (a Mexican cocktail featuring beer, spicy tomato juice, and lime) – it's the perfect way to quench your thirst as you wander the aisles.

Liked by the locals

"The swap meet is mythic in Los Angeles – it's so much more than an affordable place to shop. Swap meets are where neighborhoods create community, reaffirm identity, and build collective memories."

SAMANTA HELOU HERNANDEZ,
BILINGUAL MULTIMEDIA JOURNALIST

Home Touches

L.A. living means bright, airy spaces, artistic accents, and a constant push and pull between minimalist modern and maximalist quirk. Decorate your space with a bit of city style from these local favorites.

ROLLING GREENS

Map 4; 9528 Jefferson Boulevard, Culver City; ///areas.admiral.ramp; https://rghomeandgarden.com

Looking to up your greenery game? Pay a visit to Rolling Greens' Culver City flagship. Its design experts will help you get your home garden looking social media-ready in no time. And even if you're not all that into plants (yet), this seasonal nursery is worth a trip just to stroll around the terraced grounds. Wind your way through

Try it!
STYLE UP YOUR PLANTS

Take a hands-on class or workshop at the Rolling Greens "Arrangement Bar," where plant experts will teach you how to make wreaths, succulents, and potted plants good enough for a movie set.

blooming greenhouses, nooks filled with vintage furnishings, and an epic collection of suitably stylish containers. It's like stepping into the pages of a glossy design magazine.

HD BUTTERCUP

Map 4; 3225 Helms Avenue, Culver City; ///limes.second.page;
https://hdbuttercup.com

If you've ever dreamed of finding an indie homewares store the size of IKEA, try shopping at HD Buttercup. This 150,000-sq-ft (14,000-sq-m) design and furniture emporium is where Angelenos of all ages browse and scheme for the homes of their dreams. Classic or modern, vintage or industrial, there's bound to be something that'll suit your style.

NICK METROPOLIS COLLECTIBLES

Map 4; 1846 Adams Boulevard, Hancock Park;
///mimic.name.occurs; (323) 934-3700

It's hard to explain the oddity that is Nick Metropolis – you need to see it for yourself. To the untrained eye, this lot stuffed with oversized vintage signs, mannequins, outdoor furniture, and quirky collectibles seems a lot like a junkyard. But as West Adams locals (and Hollywood set designers) know, it's actually a treasure trove where you'll find things you never knew you wanted and now can never live without.

» Don't leave without exploring every nook and cranny. It'll take a while, but it's the only way to make sure you don't miss any hidden gems.

GOLD BUG

Map 6; 34 E. Union Street, Pasadena; ///yards.dose.fixed;
www.goldbugpasadena.com

It can get a little macabre, what with the insect taxidermy and all, but there's no doubt that Gold Bug is one of L.A.'s most distinctive home goods stores. Secreted down a side alley, with rotating collections of art, jewelry, and offbeat artifacts (think anything from $3,000 amber skulls to $20 hand-poured black candles), this modern curiosity shop is more like a shoppable museum than a boutique. It's a favorite with gift seekers, who know they'll always find something for the friend who has it all – apart from an anatomical heart lamp, of course.

» Don't leave without buying a statement piece (of any price), so you can quiz friendly owner Theodora Coleman about the artist who created it.

LEAF AND SPINE

Map 6; 5440 York Boulevard, Highland Park; ///firmly.super.holly;
(323) 257-5323

The indoor plant scene in L.A. has gone as wild as a pothos vine without a climbing guide. Seemingly every neighborhood has a store where homeworkers can get some greenery for their office, but only Highland Park has one luring plant parents from across L.A. County (and even from other states). At Leaf and Spine, owner Dustin Bulaon has curated a unique stash of aroids, succulents, and begonias that take the humble houseplant to an all-new level – some of the rare specimens here can cost hundreds of

Keep an eye on social media for the store's "plant drops," when highly sought-after species go on sale.

dollars per pot. It's the best place in town to buy a plant too expensive to kill – giving you a very good incentive to water it.

BERBERE IMPORTS

Map 4; 8728 Aviation Boulevard, Inglewood; ///love.spirit.zeal; https://berbereImports.com

Imagine the entire Silk Road flowing into a 50,000-sq-ft (4,645-sq-m) L.A. showroom, and you'll have a rough idea of what to expect at Berbere. For more than 40 years, owner Suad Cano has been using her energy and expert negotiation skills to import artisan homewares from Africa, Asia, and the Middle East. These frequent buying trips have resulted in a wonderland of a store that stocks everything from centuries-old pottery to customized Indian doors (and every Balinese Buddha statue in between).

CACTUS STORE

Map 1; 1505 1/2 Echo Park Avenue, Echo Park; ///leap.wooden.horn; https://cactus.store

At this store, the cactus is more than just a plant; it's an entire lifestyle. In the front, you'll find an indoor desert of spiky plant babies (including rare specimens and custom grows), while out back lie all the accessories you could ever want to go with them (house fertilizer, signature clay pots, and lines of embroidered clothing and outdoor furniture). Grab life by the thorns and get in on the action.

Record Stores

As the unofficial capital of the West Coast music scene, L.A. loves its records. Sure, times haven't always been easy for the city's stores, but these survivors are proof that vinyl is here to stay.

RECORD SURPLUS

Map 4; 12436 Santa Monica Boulevard, Sawtelle; ///stews.atoms.mirror; www.recordsurplusla.com

L.A. is full of gutsy risk-takers following their dreams, and Record Surplus is a prime example. In the late 2010s, when many record stores were closing, it took the brave decision to expand. The move paid off, and it's now home to one of the largest selections of new and used vinyl in town. Join deal seekers digging through stacks of jazz, soul, blues, Latin, reggae, country, hip-hop, and more.

THE RECORD PARLOUR

Map 3; 6408 Selma Avenue, Hollywood; ///short.preoccupied.judges; (323) 464-7757

Analog music lovers of the world, unite! This self-described "Emporium of 20th Century Entertainment" is vintage audio heaven – think retro signage, old-school music equipment, and crate upon crate of records. It'll take you back to a time before Spotify, when vinyl was the only way to bring music to your ears, and the local characters browsing the aisles all wore trilbies (here, many still do).

AMOEBA MUSIC
Map 3; 6200 Hollywood Boulevard, Hollywood; ///clock.behind.torn; www.amoeba.com

Cool kids want to work here, rock stars want to play here, and everyone else wants to buy records here: Amoeba Music is a true West Coast icon. Jam-packed with all the CDs, vinyl, and merch your heart could ever desire, this Hollywood store is truly huge – in fact, it's so big you need a map to navigate around. Block out an afternoon, or even a whole day, for some serious rummaging.

>> Don't leave without seeing an in-store performance. It's an honor for major musical acts to play the Amoeba stage while in L.A.

FREAKBEAT RECORDS
Map 6; 13616 Ventura Boulevard, Sherman Oaks; ///starts.flank.remark; www.freakbeatrecords.com

Quality over quantity sums up the record store scene in the San Fernando Valley – and Freakbeat leads the (small) pack. The staff here are knowledgeable music nerds who've curated a flawless selection of records, ranging across all genres, from folk to funk. Okay, you might not always find the latest big-name release here, but you'll always discover something fun and new.

FINGERPRINTS MUSIC

Map 5; 420 E. 4th Street, Long Beach; ///provide.central.stud;
www.fingerprintsmusic.com

Fingerprints casts off the classic grungy, dusty record store feel in favor of a more laid-back look: think high ceilings, exposed brick, industrial lighting, and a super-cool collection of poster art. But that's not to say it's all style over substance: the vinyl collection here is just as well curated as the decor. Rock, rap, jazz, hip-hop — you name it, Fingerprints has got it. Want to get your hands on something extra special? Time your visit here with Record Store Day. Fingerprints is the local HQ for events, and it's always got the latest exclusives.

» Don't leave without enjoying a latte or a nutritious lunch on the streetside patio at Berlin, the coffee shop and all-day bistro that stands next door.

ROCKAWAY RECORDS

Map 2; 2395 Glendale Boulevard, Silver Lake; ///poem.allow.sparks;
www.rockaway.com

This one's for all the die-hard collectors out there. Rockaway's owners, Greg and Wayne Johnson, have spent more than 40 years buying up the vinyl collections of label execs, studio engineers, and DJs, whose unwanted goods are music fan gold. Part museum, part record store (note: you'll need to make an appointment to visit), Rockaway has got enough rare vinyl, posters, gold records, instruments, and backstage passes to make even the most experienced crate diggers totally lose their cool. Always wanted a still-sealed copy of The Beatles' iconic *White Album*? How about an original *The Velvet Underground & Nico LP*, complete with banana sticker? Well, now's your chance. Heck, why not throw in a 1984 Van Halen tour tee while you're at it?

PERMANENT RECORDS
Map 2; 1906 Cypress Avenue, Cypress Park; ///salad.served.count;
www.permanentrecordsla.com

Permanent's curatorial philosophy is "all killer no filler," and it's fair to say it delivers just that. Not only does the store sell a tantalizing selection of vintage rock vinyl and obscure punk releases, but it also makes music; the store has its own independent label, putting out limited releases from local artists. And, on top of that, it has its own bar, the Roadhouse. While away a couple of hours here, rubbing shoulders with Highland Park's vintage-wearing tastemakers and music-head hipsters, flicking through the stacks of records before settling down with a beer to admire your latest finds.

Try it!
CATCH A SHOW

Why not top off some shopping with a show? At the Permanent Records Roadhouse (next door to the store), you can catch an amateur comedy show or a local band nearly any night of the week.

Book Nooks

L.A. loves a good story, so it's no surprise that the city's bookstores are thriving. If you're in need of a book for a beach day, then these spots have got you (hard)covered.

THE LAST BOOKSTORE

Map 1; 453 S. Spring Street, Downtown; ///mint.bets.wire; www.lastbookstorela.com

In 2015, when John Spencer decided to open a used bookstore in a downtown loft, he assumed that the project would fail due to the decline of the bookselling industry (hence the name). Turns out he was wrong. The Last Bookstore has since expanded into a multistory hub, becoming the largest new and used bookstore

Try it!
GO TO A POETRY SLAM

Enjoy literature brought to life with The Definitive Soapbox, a popular Slam poetry event in Long Beach. Check social media for details of the next event and the annual festival.

in California. Among its labyrinthine aisles, you'll find folks browsing for the latest bestseller, hidden nooks lined with funky artworks, and books that literally fly off the shelves in spectacular sculptural displays. How could it not have been doomed for success?

» **Don't leave without** checking out the expansive and very rad vinyl record collection on the main floor. You can't miss it.

SKYLIGHT BOOKS
Map 2; 1818 N. Vermont Avenue, Los Feliz; ///hurt.good.mice; www.skylightbooks.com

This light and airy space – complete with a leafy ficus tree in the middle – is a literary pillar of the artsy Los Feliz neighborhood. It's a great place to meet other book lovers, whether that's by getting a recommendation from the welcoming staff or making a new friend at a live reading. Oh, look out for Fanny, the bookstore cat, often found curled up in one of the cozy armchairs.

RE/ARTE CENTRO LITERARIO
Map 1; 2014 1/2 E. Cesar E. Chavez Avenue, Boyle Heights; ///toward.record.amuse; www.reartela.com

Launched by local poet Viva Padilla, this literary and art center grew out of the much-respected South L.A. literary journal *Dryland*. It's got an awesome selection of accessibly priced books by Black and Brown authors, though it's the events that really make this place a bustling community hub. Check out the calendar for a packed program of book readings, open mic nights, and movie screenings.

BOOK SOUP

**Map 3; 8818 Sunset Boulevard, West Hollywood; ///video.bleat.bright;
www.booksoup.com**

Nestled alongside the music venues and nightclubs of the iconic
Sunset Strip, Book Soup is as legendary as the rock stars who shop
here (Elton John is a loyal customer). A city stalwart since 1975, it's
filled with sweeping floor-to-ceiling bookshelves, rare books, a vast
magazine section, and limited-edition vinyl. Frequent readings from
authors and celebrities only add to the L.A. vibe.

VROMAN'S

**Map 6; 695 E. Colorado Boulevard, Pasadena; ///sits.slap.moods;
www.vromansbookstore.com**

Vroman's might be one of the oldest bookstores in Southern California
(it was founded in 1894), but it's still got a youthful buzz. In fact, it's
super child-friendly, with teen book clubs and kids' storytime, making
it a great place to visit with young ones in tow. And the best bit?
There's an in-store wine bar. Kick back with a glass and a new
page-turner while the kids are being entertained.

REPARATIONS CLUB

**Map 4; 3054 S. Victoria Avenue, West Adams; ///awake.dame.fines;
https://rep.club/m**

With its photo-ready book displays, colorful couches, and jazz
soundtrack, Rep Club is the kind of place you'll stay much longer
than expected. This intimate, Black-focused bookstore and creative

space is like a home from home, with staff who welcome you as part of the family. Even online orders come with a sweet, handwritten thank-you note.

THE RIPPED BODICE

Map 4; 3806 Main Street, Culver City; ///sharp.live.activism; www.therippedbodicela.com

Lover of love? A trip to this indie bookstore is a must. Housed in Culver City behind an unabashedly pink storefront, the suggestively named Ripped Bodice was launched by two sisters, eager to create a feminist and sex-positive space where readers could browse steamy erotica without being judged. They succeeded: pick up a tome and enjoy a raunchy read with pride.

>> Don't leave without signing up for the "Read, Romance, Repeat" subscription box, which sends a titillating book to your door every month.

TÍA CHUCHA'S CENTRO CULTURAL & BOOKSTORE

Map 6; 12677 Glenoaks Boulevard, Sylmar; ///ages.onion.pencil; www.tiachucha.org

When this store first opened in 2001, the northeast San Fernando Valley had no bookstores, art galleries, or major cultural spaces. Now, thanks to Tía Chucha's, the community not only has somewhere to buy culturally diverse books but also a thriving program of workshops and events (in both Spanish and English) to attend. A whole new creative scene from one little bookstore – not bad, eh?

Farmers' Markets

With much of the nation's food supply coming from California, it makes sense that farmers' markets are a big thing in L.A. While most are hyperlocal, here's a few that have become destinations in themselves.

MAR VISTA FARMERS' MARKET

Map 4; Venice Boulevard at Grand View Street, Mar Vista; ///status.wire.clip; www.marvistafarmersmarket.org

Set your alarm and get to this Sunday street fair early; it's the only way you're guaranteed to snag a table in the dining section. Mar Vista might look like any other modest neighborhood farmers' market, but, in fact, it's home to some of the county's most imaginative pop-up food vendors. Prepare to jostle with yogis and tech workers at stalls serving tasty plates of things like barbecue and vegan soul food.

SANTA MONICA FARMERS' MARKET

Map 4; Arizona Avenue, between 2nd and 4th streets, Santa Monica; ///wool.motor.calls; www.santamonica.gov

The granddaddy of L.A. farmers' markets, this weekly multi-block behemoth has been the place to get fresh produce since way before it was cool (read: this is the market that made it cool). Every

Wednesday morning, famous chefs and health-conscious Westsiders descend for the latest hauls of SoCal's finest fruits and vegetables. It's a feast of freshness, so make sure you bring an appetite.

» Don't leave without visiting the Weiser Farms stall, a family-owned operation that sells vegetables to many of L.A.'s top restaurants.

GRAND CENTRAL MARKET

Map 1; 317 S. Broadway, Downtown; ///casino.served.trader;
www.grandcentralmarket.com

L.A. is constantly reinventing itself, and Grand Central Market is no exception. One of the fanciest markets on the West Coast when it opened in 1917, it later became known as a cheap spot to pick up some produce or a grab-and-go lunch. Nowadays, it's on its third incarnation as a lively destination for chef-driven food (shout out to Eggslut, Sticky Rice, and Sarita's Pupuseria), forever bustling with hungry foodies. Who knows where it will take things next.

LONG BEACH SOUTHEAST CERTIFIED FARMERS' MARKET

Map 5; 2nd Street and N. Marina Drive, Long Beach;
///whips.collects.city; www.goodveg.org/sunday-long-beach-southeast

Shopping in the sun is always a treat, but it's even better with the waft of a cool sea breeze. This oceanside Sunday pop-up – "The Marina Market" to regulars – is the perfect place to browse without working up a sweat. Pro tip: grab some baked goods and fresh fruit and picnic at the nearby marina, overlooking the splashy boats.

THE ORIGINAL FARMERS' MARKET

Map 3; 6333 W. 3rd Street, Fairfax; ///scarcely.chops.pull;
www.farmersmarketla.com

First a place for farmers to sell produce from their trucks, this L.A. staple has grown into a maze of built-in stalls hawking everything from fresh pastries to meat to ice cream. The best bit? It's permanent, so you can shop here seven days a week.

» **Don't leave without** buying a hot lunch at one of the food counters. Our pick is the Gumbo Pot, serving a mix of Cajun specialties.

STUDIO CITY FARMERS' MARKET

Map 6; Ventura Place, Studio City; ///remind.played.steer;
www.studiocityfarmersmarket.com

Meeting friends with kids? Head to this Sunday San Fernando Valley farmers' market. Little ones are kept busy by the play area, climbing wall, and bounce house, so you'll be able to, you know, actually make purchases without all their adorable distractions.

HOLLYWOOD FARMERS' MARKET

Map 3; Selma and Ivar, Hollywood; ///nest.renew.kinds;
www.seela.org/markets-hollywood

Think Hollywood and the tourist trap that is the Walk of Fame probably comes to mind. Beyond that, though, is a flourishing community with some pockets of serious cool – like this Sunday pop-up. It features produce stalls and funky artisans like Marianne's Clay Creations, as well as one-of-a-kind food vendors like Marcie's Pies. Yum.

Liked by the locals

"More than anywhere else, the farmers' markets in L.A. really highlight ingredients at the peak of their season. There's always something unique and exciting to play with, things you've never heard of, like apriums – that's apricot plus plum."

MELISSA ORTIZ,
EXECUTIVE CHEF, ROSE PARK ON PINE

EAST 7TH STREET

CHERRY AVENUE

JUNIPERO AVENUE

EAST 6TH STREET

Dig for treasure at
ASSISTANCE LEAGUE THRIFT STORE

It's hard to resist this volunteer-run thrift store, which bursts at the seams with carefully curated clothing and home goods at affordable prices.

Coast into
PIGEON'S ROLLER SKATE SHOP

Nowhere celebrates SoCal's roller-skate scene like this one-stop shop. Make like it's the 90s and get fitted for a colorful pair of quads by experts from the local derby scene.

EAST 4TH STREET

Support small businesses at
THE HANGOUT

Get lost in this modern take on an antiques mall. You'll find stalls selling unique vintage finds, plus books and records.

Go crate-digging at
THIRD EYE RECORDS

For the record: Third Eye is *the* place to go for preloved vinyl. Chat to owner Gary, who is only too happy to recommend a band or artist.

CHERRY AVENUE

JUNIPERO AVENUE

WISCONSIN AVENUE

EAST 3RD STREET

0 meters 200
0 yards 200

EAST 7TH STREET

TEMPLE

AVENUE

Pick up a rad read at PAGE AGAINST THE MACHINE
Dip into one of Long Beach's newer independent bookstores, a punny ode to the owner's proclivity for radical reads, zines, and alternative thinking.

Baker Arturo Enciso used to sell all manner of bread and pastries from his living room before opening **Gusto Bread** *in August 2020.*

A morning shopping on
Retro Row

Angelenos have been shopping for vintage fashion long before it was cool. And their thrifting go-to? That's 4th Street in Long Beach, also known as Retro Row, thanks to the slew of kitsch vintage stores that opened here in the 1990s. Today, this homey street is lined with locally owned independent shops and boutiques, as well as retro stores, of course. Grab a tote and take a morning stroll down this well-trodden street, stocking up on goodies for your home and closet.

1. Assistance League Thrift Store
2100 E. 4th Street;
www.assistanceleague.org/long-beach
///panics.drum.sheets

2. The Hangout
2122 E. 4th Street;
www.shopthehangout.com
///giggled.scales.steep

3. Pigeon's Roller Skate Shop
2148 E. 4th Street;
www.pigeonskates.com
///using.massing.however

4. Third Eye Records
2234 E. 4th Street; www.thirdeyerecordshop.com
///doctors.breath.snuggle

5. Page Against the Machine
2714 E. 4th Street;
www.patmbooks.com
///user.hesitate.froze

Gusto Bread ///crystal.servants.stored

EAST 3RD STREET

TEMPLE

AVENUE

ARTS & CULTURE

Lights, camera, action! L.A. is, of course, the home of movie magic, but it also has a diverse cultural scene that ranges from quirky museums to thought-provoking art.

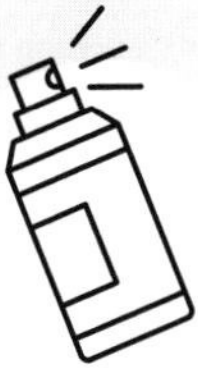

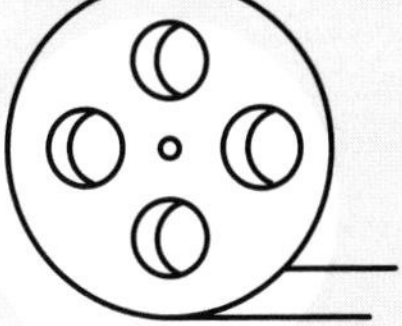

City History

Throughout L.A.'s short history, countless communities and movements have found a home here, resulting in a rich past (and present) that's represented at these important spots.

RANCHO LOS ALAMITOS

Map 5; 6400 E. Bixby Hill Road, Long Beach;
///version.unrealistic.rapport; www.rancholosalamitos.com

Farming probably isn't the first industry you associate with L.A., but in fact it's been part of the city's economy for centuries. At this historic ranch, you can get a taste of 19th-century agricultural life (complete with barnyard animals) – and learn about the Indigenous Tongva-Gabrielino people, who were displaced by the farm's founders.

ONE GALLERY

Map 3; 626 N. Robertson Boulevard, West Hollywood;
///rents.honest.faded; www.onearchives.org

There's more to L.A.'s queer culture than WeHo's famous bars and clubs. Protests against LGBTQ+ discrimination date back to the 1960s, and the queer publication *The Advocate* was founded here in 1967. Today, the city is home to the largest collection of LGBTQ+

materials in the world – the ONE Archives at the University of Southern California Libraries – which are curated into rotating exhibitions at this partner space. Past topics have ranged from AIDS activism to queer Chicanx artists of the 1960s–90s.

JAPANESE AMERICAN NATIONAL MUSEUM

Map 1; 100 N. Central Avenue, Little Tokyo ///diary.reap.stream; www.janm.org

Founded in 1985, this museum was the brainchild of a group of World War II veterans and Little Tokyo businessmen, eager to preserve the history of Japanese Americans in the city – one of its early exhibitions encouraged locals to share their stories of being forcibly relocated to internment camps during the war. Popular with history buffs, it's also an inspiring space for creative thinkers, with changing exhibits on celebrated artists and topics like Japanese tattoo traditions.

MARIACHI PLAZA

Map 1; 1831 1st Street, Boyle Heights ///urgent.bills.since

Mexican culture is an integral part of L.A. life – around 30 percent of the city's population has Mexican ancestry – and it's kept alive and well in Boyle Heights. In a tradition that began in the 1930s, elegant mariachi musicians gather at this square to showcase their talents in the hope of being hired for paying gigs.

» Don't leave without getting a meal at Birrieria Don Boni, a casual joint that specializes in tender birria (stewed goat).

CALIFORNIA AFRICAN AMERICAN MUSEUM (CAAM)

Map 4; 600 State Drive, Exposition Park; ///divisions.deny.advice;
https://caamuseum.org

Black people have been shaping Los Angeles from its inception –
like Biddy Mason, who got her freedom from enslavement in the
early 1850s and went on to become a successful businesswoman in
local real estate. Her story is just one of many that's been shared at this
fascinating museum, which focuses on Black culture, history, and
visual art in California and the West. It's the kind of space best explored
with a friend: the exhibits have a knack for being cleverly thought-
provoking, and you'll want a buddy to chew them over with.

EL PUEBLO DE LOS ANGELES

Map 1; 125 Paseo de la Plaza, Downtown; ///landed.models.strain https://
elpueblo.lacity.org

Without the El Pueblo district, there would be no L.A. – it was here
that the City of Angels was born, founded in 1781 by Mexican settlers
on the land of the Chumash and Tongva peoples. And without
Christine Sterling, there wouldn't be the El Pueblo that we know today.
A wealthy white Californian, she led a campaign in the 1920s to save
the area from demolition and also established the "traditional"
Mexican marketplace on Olvera Street. Despite being created for
Anglo visitors (and glossing over issues of colonization), the area has
become a vibrant cultural center for the city's Mexican community.

» **Don't leave without** visiting the Chinese American Museum on
N. Los Angeles Street, housed in a building constructed in 1890.

Liked by the locals

"Black culture is thriving in Los Angeles, and CAAM is a critical hub to explore it, presenting work by dynamic artists and scholars in a space that has for decades been dedicated to this vision. I think you sense that history when you enter our galleries."

CAMERON SHAW, EXECUTIVE DIRECTOR AT THE
CALIFORNIA AFRICAN AMERICAN MUSEUM

Favorite Museums

Few places celebrate L.A.'s endless creativity better than the city's artsy museums. Ranging from the strange to the sublime, these inventive spaces are our top picks.

MUSEUM OF NEON ART

Map 2; 216 S. Brand Boulevard, Glendale; ///actual.turns.stack;
www.neonmona.org

Follow the call of the brightly lit diver atop this museum and plunge into a quirky collection of neon and kinetic pieces. Vintage items trace the history of neon signs (including the use of questionable cultural stereotypes), while contemporary examples showcase the exciting future of this electrifying art (pun firmly intended).

MUSEUM OF JURASSIC TECHNOLOGY

Map 4; 9341 Venice Boulevard, Culver City; ///with.items.puzzle;
www.mjt.org

No description can truly capture the magic of this place, which is just as bewildering as its name makes it sound. Inside, you'll discover a mysterious world of dimly lit displays that include "The Lives of Perfect Creatures: Dogs of the Soviet Space Program" and the

Head to the museum's leafy rooftop garden to enjoy some sun while surrounded by chirping birds.

miniature work of Hagop Sandaldjian, which features Disney characters standing on top of needles. It's a bizarre cabinet of curiosities treasured by Angelenos.

CRAFT CONTEMPORARY

Map 3; 5814 Wilshire Boulevard, Mid-Wilshire; ///monday.coats.saves; www.craftcontemporary.org

Can't get the creative juices flowing? Pop to Craft Contemporary for a hit of inspiration. It's always got something new and cool going on – like the time its exterior was covered in 15,000 crochet granny squares by Yarn Bombing Los Angeles. Exhibitions cover all types of innovative craft practices, from ceramics and weaving to video art.

» Don't leave without visiting the gift shop, which offers thoughtfully curated items such as ceramics, books, and textiles.

MUSEUM OF LATIN AMERICAN ART

Map 5; 628 Alamitos Avenue, Long Beach; ///found.official.formally; https://molaa.org

Fun fact: back in the 1920s, what is now the main entrance area of this museum functioned as a roller-skating rink. The speeding skaters have long gone, but the space lives on for laid-back artsy types who pass lazy afternoons in the galleries here. A few even skip the collection and head straight to the Robert Gumbiner Sculpture & Events Garden – with its bright pink walls and outdoor artworks, it's an ideal place to soak up the sun or doodle in a sketchbook.

Solo, Pair, Crowd

Exploring an epic art collection is always fun with the right company (even if that's just your sketchbook).

FLYING SOLO
Take your time

The largest art museum on the West Coast, the encyclopedic L.A. County Museum of Art (LACMA) is perfect for introspective art lovers who want to explore multiple exhibitions alone with their thoughts.

IN A PAIR
Downtown date

With its casual-yet-cool downtown setting, the Broad Museum is a great date option. Swap life stories as you admire contemporary artworks from household names like Kara Walker and Jeff Koons.

FOR A CROWD
Family-friendly fun

Not only does The Getty have an amazing art collection, but it also has the picturesque Central Garden. This means plenty of outdoor space for kids to roam around — and there's beer and wine on-site for the adults, too.

VINCENT PRICE ART MUSEUM

Map 6; 1301 Avenida Cesar Chavez, Monterey Park;
///gates.detail.happy; http://vincentpriceartmuseum.org

In a plot twist you might not have seen coming from the name, this isn't a museum filled with artworks by (or of) horror-movie icon Vincent Price. In fact, it gets its moniker because the collection was started by Price and his wife Mary Grant, who donated some of their personal artworks to East Los Angeles College. Now a fully fledged art institution, it draws a diverse mix of antique art lovers (it's famed for its pieces from the Ancient Americas) and cutting-edge creatives checking out the contemporary Latinx art shows.

» Don't leave without exploring work by local artists and makers at the nearby Plaza de la Raza cultural center.

ACADEMY MUSEUM

Map 3; 6067 Wilshire Boulevard, Mid-Wilshire; ///space.outer.gets;
www.academymuseum.org

As the home of Hollywood, L.A. is synonymous with the movie industry. It's only fitting, then, that the city is also the location of the country's largest museum on the subject. (And it's a suitably glitzy one, too, with a larger-than-life globe-shaped theater designed by Renzo Piano.) The whole place is a cinephile's dream – the core exhibition, where you can meet the actual E.T.; the exclusive products in the gift shop (like vinyl soundtracks curated by Amoeba Music, *p93*); and the state-of-the-art theaters where you can catch a movie. There's even a chance to experience what it's like to win an Oscar – just make sure you've prepped your acceptance speech.

Public Art

L.A. is a city of spectacle, and its streets and public spaces are no exception. You'll find amazing art in every corner of town, often bringing social commentary as well as color.

WATTS TOWERS

Map 5; 1727 E. 107th Street, Watts; ///successes.basin.orders; www.wattstowers.org

Sometimes, art is simply about the joy of creating. Begun in 1921, this now-iconic installation on a street in Watts was the passion project of Italian American Sabato "Simon" Rodia. For no other reason than the heck of it, he constructed the multicolored towers over the course of three decades. The end result looks like a mini Sagrada Familia, built entirely out of recycled materials.

URBAN LIGHT

Map 3; 5905 Wilshire Boulevard, Mid-Wilshire; ///rocket.army.flats; https://collections.lacma.org/node/214966

Every major city has a large-scale art installation that's social media gold, and Chris Burden's *Urban Light* is just that for L.A. (Yes that does mean you'll be competing with wannabe influencers for the best view.) It features rows of street lamps gathered from across Southern California, which turn on automatically when the sun sets. The effect is magical, and perfect fodder for twinkly nighttime shots.

» Don't leave without looking closely at the details of each lamp; some include small rosebuds as decoration.

THE GREAT WALL OF LOS ANGELES
Map 6; 12900 Oxnard Street, North Hollywood; ///loud.candy.achieving; https://planning.lacity.org/blog/great-wall-los-angeles

Not one to shy from a challenge, in 1976 local artist Judy Baca embarked on a project to transform a concrete flood control channel into something vibrant and colorful. With the help of the local community and at-risk youth, what started as a 1,000-ft (300-m) mural has since more than doubled — making it the largest of its kind in the world. Its numerous panels tell the history of California, with a conscious emphasis on marginalized and Indigenous communities.

THE WALL PROJECT
Map 3; 5900 Wilshire Boulevard, Mid-Wilshire; ///bikes.roses.human; www.wendemuseum.org/programs/wall-project

L.A. has plenty of "drive too quickly and you'll miss it" public art moments, and this is one of them. Installed near nondescript office buildings on Wilshire Boulevard are 10 painted panels of the Berlin Wall, commissioned by the Wende Museum to celebrate the 20th anniversary of the wall's fall. Join lunching museum workers and field trip groups in giving the works the appreciation they deserve.

MURAL MILE

**Map 6; Van Nuys Boulevard, Pacoima; ///terms.drank.learn;
www.muralmile.org**

The Walk of Fame isn't the only place you'll find famous faces in the
city; this collection of artworks in Pacoima features homages to figures
like actor Danny Trejo, activist Assata Shakur, and musician Ritchie
Valens. Launched by artist Levi Ponce, who felt there wasn't enough
art around the neighborhood, Mural Mile is actually more extensive
than the name suggests. It comprises over 50 murals in a 3-mile
(5-km) radius, often in places where you might not expect them – like
the back of the Pacoima Entrepreneurial Center, where a huge piece
by Germs explodes with color and references to Mexican heritage.

AMÉRICA TROPICAL MURAL

**Map 1; 125 Paseo de la Plaza, Downtown; ///grabs.player.elite;
https://theamericatropical.org**

In 1932, when La Plaza Art Center commissioned Mexican artist
David Alfaro Siqueiros to create a public artwork on a "Tropical
America" theme, it was expecting a pleasantly idyllic scene. Instead,
it got a mural depicting a crucified Indigenous Mexican figure, overtly
referencing imperialism and the racist treatment of marginalized
groups. Swiftly whitewashed to avoid upsetting tourists at the
romanticized Mexican marketplace on Olvera Street, the work was
all but forgotten until its rediscovery in the 1960s. Today, you can
join artists and political activists in paying tribute to the carefully
restored mural and learn more about its controversial past at the
América Tropical Interpretive Center.

LONG BEACH WALLS

Map 5; start at 927 Pine Avenue, Long Beach; ///reported.rejects.retire;
www.powwowlongbeach.com

For one week every summer, Long Beach hosts the international POW! WOW! street art festival. That's great in itself – there are lots of fun pop-up events – but the best part is the legacy that the festival leaves behind. Fresh murals are added each year, so the whole city is being steadily turned into a walkable (or bikeable) art gallery. Why not get your steps in while doing a self-guided tour? Our favorite stops include the characterful posse of panda bears on Pine Avenue by Woes and Hilda Palafox's colorful beachgoers on Redondo Avenue.

» **Don't leave without** keeping an eye out for utility boxes painted by local artists – they're dotted around the city as part of a local program to decorate traffic signal controller cabinets.

L.A. HISTORY: A MEXICAN PERSPECTIVE

Map 4; Natural History Museum of Los Angeles County, 900 W. Exposition
Boulevard, Exposition Park; ///twice.branch.sector; https://nhm.org

Art has the power to spark tough conversations, and this is one of those pieces that proves it. Censored for its warts-and-all depiction of L.A.'s history – including events like the Zoot Suit Riots, the death of Ruben Salazar during the 1970 National Chicano Moratorium March, and the internment of Japanese communities during World War II – Barbara Carrasco's 1981 mural is now back on display for all to see in the Welcome Center of the Natural History Museum.

Architectural Landmarks

L.A. doesn't have just one building style – everyone from mid-century modernists to Spanish colonial revivalists have come here to build their dreams. These boundary-pushing buildings tell the story of L.A.

HOLLYHOCK HOUSE

Map 2; 4800 Hollywood Boulevard, Vermont; ///leap.villa.vine; www.barnsdall.org/hollyhock-house

The first house Frank Lloyd Wright designed in L.A., Hollyhock House was intended as a home for oil heiress Aline Barnsdall (hollyhock was her favorite flower and is a recurring motif throughout the building).

Try it!
MUSEUM ROW

Go on a DIY architecture tour with a walk along Wilshire Boulevard's Museum Row. The buildings along this mile-long strip range from classical (LACMA) to ultra-modern (Petersen Automotive Museum).

The pair's relationship soured, however, when Wright took too long to complete the over-budget project, and Barnsdall refused to live in it. Instead she donated the hilltop palace to the city, to the delight of the many design lovers found noseying around inside.

UNION STATION

Map 1; 800 N. Alameda Street, Downtown; ///youth.appeal.plus; www.unionstationla.com

As one of the last great railroad stations built in the U.S. (in 1939), Union Station is a celebrated piece of history. The Spanish-style building predates the popularity of cars in Los Angeles (hard to imagine now, we know) and was the first stop for countless folks arriving to live their California Dream. Grab an iced coffee and ponder this past, in a quiet spot away from the downtown commuters.

WAYFARERS CHAPEL

Map 5; 5755 Palos Verdes Drive S., Palos Verdes; ///filtering.conflicting.yelp; www.wayfarerschapel.org

Picture a glittering glass church, nestled in a patch of redwood trees on a scenic bluff right next to the coast. That's the Wayfarers Chapel in a nutshell, and it's every bit as romantic as it sounds. Unsurprisingly, the light and airy building is hugely popular with lovebirds as a wedding venue. But anyone can come and enjoy the space while it's unoccupied, for their own moment of heavenly bliss.

» **Don't leave without** snapping your next profile picture in the verdant rose garden behind the chapel.

THE DONUT HOLE

**Map 6; 15300 Amar Road, La Puente; ///goal.kettles.beeline;
(626) 968-2912**

Programmatic architecture – where structures are designed to
look like what they sell – has got to be one of L.A.'s most weird-yet-
wonderful building styles. There are dozens of donut-shaped donut
shops in the city, but this one in the Latinx enclave of La Puente
is a fun drive-through variation on the theme. Built in 1968, it's
comprised of two 26-ft- (8-m-) wide fiberglass donuts connected
by a tunnel, which you drive your car through to pick up your
order. It's one of the most photographed bakeries in the U.S.,
with people coming from far and wide to get snaps for their
social media feeds.

» Don't leave without treating yourself to some donuts, naturally.
We recommend a box of the mini glazed cronuts – they're soft, fluffy,
and utterly delicious.

SCHINDLER HOUSE

**Map 3; 35 N. Kings Road, West Hollywood; ///blues.fields.crops;
https://makcenter.org/sites/schindler-house**

Said to be the first-ever house built in the modernist style, this
sprawling commune was designed by Austrian architect Robert
Schindler. Intended to house two families, the glass-and-concrete
structure was built with no bedrooms or dining rooms, pioneering
an open-concept floor plan that was groundbreaking in California
architecture when it was erected in the early 1920s. It can be
hard to appreciate just how revolutionary this was while touring

Check the online calendar for special events at Schindler House, like art shows and lectures.

the interior today – everyone's doing it now, of course – but that doesn't stop the building from being any less beautiful.

THE GAMBLE HOUSE

Map 6; 4 Westmoreland Place, Pasadena; ///boat.outfit.oasis;
https://gamblehouse.org

Prepare for some serious house envy: this is the custom, exquisitely hand-crafted home of your dreams. Designed by iconic architecture firm Greene & Greene, it deftly combines Japanese and Californian aesthetics, blending teak, maple, and oak surfaces with low-slung roofs reminiscent of pagodas. It's one of the finest examples of Arts and Crafts architecture in the U.S., even making it onto the National Register of Historic Places.

LOS ANGELES CENTRAL LIBRARY

Map 1; 630 W. 5th Street, Downtown; ///stocks.dollar.third;
www.lapl.org

Built in the 1920s, this historic library is a veritable Art Deco temple to books and learning – it even comes complete with a colorful, sunburst-tiled pyramid at its crown. Inside, the most striking room is the sumptuous Rotunda, decorated with murals depicting the (extremely romanticized) history of California and a gilded, stained-glass globe known as the Zodiac Chandelier. Because you can never have too much Tinseltown glitz, right?

Movie Theaters

In a city that birthed the film industry as we know it, you better believe that the places showing movies are destinations in themselves. Here, theaters are part art gallery, part performance space, and part town square.

EGYPTIAN THEATRE

Map 3; 6712 Hollywood Boulevard, Hollywood; ///stiff.rewarding.bank; www.americancinematheque.com

Even if you're not likely to be invited to walk a red carpet anytime soon, you can still pretend by buying a ticket for the theater that housed the first-ever Hollywood premiere (black tie is completely optional). Renovated in 2022 by Netflix, this iconic space positively oozes Golden Age glamour, with a signature Egyptian theme that includes four large columns at the front, plus vivid hieroglyphics.

VISTA THEATRE

Map 2; 4473 Sunset Drive, Los Feliz; ///Unity.shape.laser; www.vintagecinemas.com

A vintage movie house that first opened in the 1920s, the Vista has more character than most indie theaters. There's the kitschy décor for one thing, not to mention a colorful past that includes screening

Pause out front to admire an eclectic collection of cement handprints that rivals the Chinese Theatre. | adult offerings until a retool in 1980. Purchased by Quentin Tarantino in 2021, it's now a space for literal film fans, screening movies on celluloid only.

NEW BEVERLY CINEMA

Map 3; 7165 Beverly Boulevard, Fairfax; ///shovels.gentle.couch; https://thenewbev.com

Even though the surrounding neighborhood has evolved to become a bit pricey, at the New Bev you can enjoy daily double features for just the cost of a single ticket. Quentin Tarantino (yep, him again) famously saved this historic theater when he purchased it in 2007; L.A.'s industry nerds still line up for its bill of B-movie, Old Hollywood, and newer offerings curated by the film-obsessed director.

» Don't leave without catching a midnight screening on a Friday of a movie from Tarantino's personal collection.

CINESPIA AT THE HOLLYWOOD FOREVER CEMETERY

Map 2; 6000 Santa Monica Boulevard; ///draw.crowned.chops; https://cinespia.org

Watching a film in a cemetery might sound strange, but it makes sense when you're in the final resting place of screen luminaries like Judy Garland and Burt Reynolds. Coming to this summer pop-up is an L.A. rite of passage: bring a bottle of wine, and settle onto the grass alongside eager first-timers and nostaligic old hands.

THE FORD

Map 3; 2580 Cahuenga Boulevard E, Hollywood Hills;
///both.posts.lined; www.theford.com

On the screen in front of you is a beloved classic; all around are the Hollywood Hills; and above you twinkle more stars than you'll ever see on the Walk of Fame. This outdoor venue feels a world away from the city, and yet at the same time it's quintessentially L.A.

ELECTRIC DUSK DRIVE-IN

Map 2; 236 N. Central Avenue, Glendale; ///cones.trunk.paused;
www.electricduskdrivein.com

It's true: Angelenos love their cars just as much as their movies. So of course this drive-in is one of the city's most popular screening experiences. Operating year-round, its program has something for everyone, from horror favorites to family-friendly gems.

THE FRIDA CINEMA

Map 6; 305 E 4th Street, Santa Ana; ///email.runs.pausing;
https://thefridacinema.org

This arthouse destination is one for true cinephiles. Yes, you'll have to cross the Orange Curtain into neighboring Orange County, but the double-screen theater in Santa Ana is a bonafide gem. It's got some of the best indie cinema programming in all of SoCal, including an impressive selection from Latinx filmmakers.

» Don't leave without exploring the rest of Santa Ana. This vibrant city is quickly becoming a new art, culture, and nightlife destination.

Liked by the locals

"We're a needle in a haystack
in terms of arts and culture in
Orange County. But I'm very
proud of the scene that we have
created, basically from scratch."

TREVOR DILLON, PROGRAMMING DIRECTOR
AT FRIDA CINEMA

Indie Art Spaces

Angelenos love to express themselves through art, and new talent is emerging here all the time. Check out these intimate art spaces, and you might just discover the next big name.

SELF-HELP GRAPHICS & ART

Map 1; 1300 E. 1st Street, East Los Angeles; ///orange.acute.debate; www.selfhelpgraphics.com

In 1970, four printmakers, frustrated by the lack of facilities for young Chicanx artists, began creating works in an East Los Angeles garage. Fast-forward 50 years, and Self-Help Graphics is now one of the city's most important destinations for Latinx and Chicanx art. Rotating exhibits offer insight into the organization's printmaking

Try it!
TAKE A CLASS

Inspired by the prints you've seen at Self-Help Graphics & Art? Then why not sign up for one of its workshops. Budding artists can try their hand at everything from silkscreen printing to rug weaving.

projects, but this is more than just a gallery space. There's also a long-standing focus on community engagement – its annual Día de los Muertos celebration attracts thousands of Angelenos.

ART + PRACTICE

Map 4; 3401 W. 43rd Place, Leimert Park; ///junior.moment.chains; www.artandpractice.org

Not content with simply being a successful international artist, Mark Bradford is giving back to his childhood community as a founder of Art + Practice. It's a unique nonprofit foundation that supports foster youth, as well as providing this free public art gallery for locals. A welcoming space focusing on artists of color, it makes a great stop on a stroll around the historic Black neighborhood of Leimert Park.

» Don't leave without stopping at nearby Hot & Cool Cafe *(p61)* to drink smoothies and snack on tasty vegan food.

LOS ANGELES CONTEMPORARY EXHIBITIONS (LACE)

Map 3; 6522 Hollywood Boulevard, Hollywood; ///vows.wrong.garden; https://welcometolace.org

You never know quite what you're going to find at LACE, but you can bet your bottom dollar it will be something genre-bending and experimental. Founded in 1978 by a group of artists, the space holds shows that range from playful to political to thought-provoking (and sometimes all three). Past highlights include a performance by Colectivo AM that encouraged the audience to join a dance party.

SHULAMIT NAZARIAN

Map 3; 616 N. La Brea Avenue, Fairfax; ///manual.crass.senses; www.shulamitnazarian.com

An oasis of calm amid the bustle of Fairfax, Shulamit Nazarian is always showing something cool. On-the-pulse art lovers swing by after brunch, eager to check out the latest mix of paintings, textile pieces, sculptures, and installations. Expect deep themes like immigrant identity and the artist's private self.

RESIDENCY ART GALLERY

Map 4; 310 E. Queen Street, Inglewood; ///piles.backs.fish; https://residencyart.com

While many art institutions across L.A. are feeling the pressure to show more artists of color without tokenizing them, spaces like Residency are proving that it's really not all that hard. Local names whose work has appeared here include Texas Isaiah, the first trans

Shh!

An industrial area of Downtown is probably not the first place you'd expect to find a cutting-edge gallery, yet here the huge Corey Helford Gallery *(https://coreyhelfordgallery.com)* is. It focuses on genres like pop surrealism and graffiti, with pieces that are often bold, intricate, and mischievous. Exhibitions include themed group shows as well as solo showcases for local talent or international names.

photographer to shoot a cover for *Vogue*, and painter Kohshin Finley, whose portraits of his friends and family have an almost photographic quality. The minimal space keeps the focus on the artwork, so you can give it the time and appreciation it deserves.

BAND OF VICES

Map 4; 5351 W. Adams Boulevard, West Adams; ///gather.claps.indoor; www.bandofvices.com

You can't miss the bright pink exterior of this West Adams exhibition space. It's an unapologetic color that chimes perfectly with the gallery's vocal intention to give a platform to historically overlooked creative communities. It's clearly something that people are eager to see more of, as there's now a second Band of Vices space just up the road – this one may have a more muted black façade, but the art inside is no less eye-catching.

HUMAN RESOURCES

Map 1; 410 Cottage Home Street, Chinatown; ///lease.bucks.inform; www.h-r.la

Ready to get conceptual? This not-for-profit space at the corner of a mostly residential block showcases contemporary art that pushes the envelope. On any given day, it could be screening a film, hosting a performance, staging a listening party, or serving as the backdrop for a music video. It's anything but traditional and that's why we love it.

>> Don't leave without calling at Sesame LA, a charming store selling everything from Asian food essentials to handmade ceramics.

0 meters 400
0 yards 400

Brookside Golf Club
was designed by famed golf architect William P. Bell in the 1920s. The 36-hole course is famed for its incredible views.

FREEWAY

FOOTHILL

LINCOLN AVENUE

ROSEMONT AVENUE

6

Stroll around THE ROSE BOWL

End your tour by exploring the most famous venue in college football history. Designed by architect Myron Hunt, the 1922 structure was inspired by ancient colliseums and can host up to 100,000 fans.

SECO STREET

Marvel at MILLARD HOUSE

Bookseller Alice Millard commissioned Frank Lloyd Wright to build this house, now known as "La Miniatura." It's very different from his Prairie style, with patterned concrete blocks creating a striking entrance.

5

PROSPECT BLVD

ROSEMONT AVENUE

Brookside Park

LINDA VISTA AVENUE

NORTH ORANGE GROVE BLVD

Stop by the UNITARIAN CHURCH

The American Craftsman porch here is lovely. Take it in before popping into the reflective sanctuary, designed by Pasadena-born Whitney R. Smith in the 1970s.

ARROYO TERRACE

Join a tour at THE GAMBLE HOUSE

Explore the neighborhood's most iconic Greene & Greene house, which is Japanese in style. *Back to the Future* fans will recognize the facade as Doc Brown's house.

4

3

2

1

Sneak a peek at the JAMES A. CULBERTSON HOUSE

Poke your head through the fence of this 1902 gem, built by Arts and Crafts architects Charles and Henry Greene for their loyal client, James A. Culbertson. The English-inspired house draws heavily on the works of designer William Morris.

Start at the MYRON HUNT RESIDENCE

Scope out the house of Rose Bowl stadium architect Myron Hunt. A long-time Pasadena resident, Myron built this frankly gorgeous house in 1905.

An afternoon admiring
architecture in Pasadena

In the early 1900s, Pasadena became an epicenter of the American Arts and Crafts (or Craftsman) movement. With the city's population growing, new homes were in demand, giving architects the opportunity to run free. The result? Beautiful, decorative, and functional houses, not dissimilar to those designed by fellow Arts and Crafts architects in Britain in the late 1800s. See them for yourself on this dreamy walking tour – just get ready for some major house envy.

1. Myron Hunt Residence
200 N. Grand Avenue
///fear.zone.axed

2. James A. Culbertson House
235 N. Grand Avenue
///forms.error.elaborate

3. Unitarian Church
1 Westmoreland Place;
www.neighborhooduu.org
///counts.shade.quest

4. The Gamble House
4 Westmoreland Place;
https://gamblehouse.org
///boat.outfit.oasis

5. Millard House
645 Prospect Crescent
///bottle.stay.tanks

6. The Rose Bowl
1001 Rose Bowl Drive
///bill.both.treat

Brookside Golf Club ///snows.oiled.values

MOUNTAIN STREET

AVENUE

OAKS

FAIR

MAPLE STREET

FREEWAY

VENTURA

PASADENA

NIGHTLIFE

As the sun sets over the Hollywood Hills, the fun is just getting started. Musicians hit the stage, comedians perfect their punch lines, and the city's revelers dance until dawn.

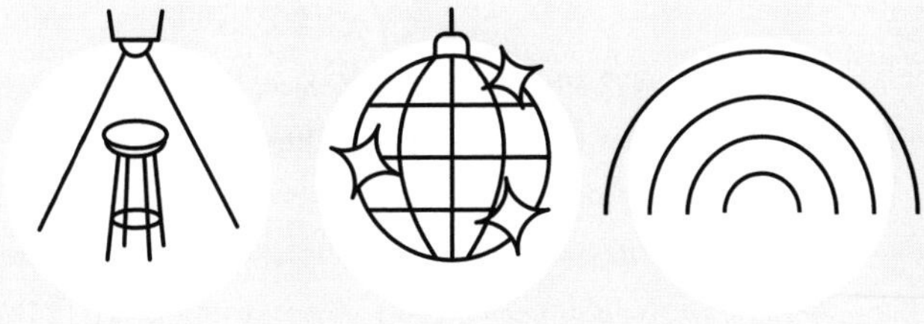

Dinner and a Show

Everything in Los Angeles is a performance, even dinner – here, you don't just get a meal but a full night of entertainment. Dress to impress, bring an appetite, and prepare to expect the unexpected.

CICADA CLUB

Map 1; 617 S. Olive Street, Downtown; ///frame.crowds.incomes; www.cicadaclub.com

If you've ever fantasized about attending a glamorous Old Hollywood party, dream no more: this swanky supper club will transport you straight back to L.A.'s 1920s heyday. Put on your best vintage glad rags, step inside the lavish Art Deco building, and join swingin' revelers dining on tasty Italian food and dancing the night away to live brass bands.

HARVELLE'S

Map 4; 1432 4th Street, Santa Monica; ///weedy.belly.normal; https://santamonica.harvelles.com

Okay, we're cheating a little bit with this one – Harvelle's doesn't actually serve its own food, but it does let you bring in takeout from the surrounding restaurants. This is dinner and a show

Tickets for Harvelle's are cheaper than at other venues, though most shows here have a two-drink minimum. dive-style: moody red lighting, cozy tables, and a rough-and-ready mix of comedy, live music, and titillating burlesque performances.

THE MAGIC CASTLE

Map 3; 7001 Franklin Avenue, Hollywood; ///urgent.throw.stones; www.magiccastle.com

Just getting inside this enigmatic clubhouse involves a magic trick – invites are issued by members only. Our advice? Check the lineup and email one of the magicians to ask (nicely) if they can put you on the guest list. Obviously we can't reveal the Magic Castle's secrets, but we can say that dinner and an exclusive show here is one of Hollywood's most memorable nights out.

» Don't leave without popping into Houdini's chamber, which is filled with memorabilia and supposedly still haunted by his ghost.

EL CID

Map 2; 4212 Sunset Boulevard, Silver Lake; ///grow.bonus.strut; www.elcidsunset.com

Pal in need of a pick-me-up? Treat them to a night in Spain at this restaurant and flamenco club. As the dancers clack and twirl across the stage, you'll get to kick back with a glass of sangria and feast on Spanish classics like tapas and paella. Once the show is over, slide across to the pretty outdoor patio where you can catch up over cocktails under the stars.

Solo, Pair, Crowd

Dinner and a show is always great for date night, but there are also plenty of options if you're on your own or with some pals.

FLYING SOLO
Jazz night

With its low-key setting, Dresden is a perfect spot to catch a show on your own or meet new people. Movie fans may recognize it as the location where Ron Burgundy (Will Ferrell) performed his jazz flute in *Anchorman*.

IN A PAIR
Old-school romance

Get a taste of classic Hollywood with an old-fashioned date at Miceli's. Here, twinkly lights and singing waitstaff will have you and your partner re-creating that spaghetti scene from *Lady and the Tramp*.

FOR A CROWD
Spooky supper

If you're in need of a scare fix before next Halloween, Beetle House is the place to go. This spooky Tim Burton-themed dinner theater experience is especially fun if you're in a group.

SADDLE RANCH CHOP HOUSE
Map 3; 8371 Sunset Boulevard, West Hollywood; ///clean.brand.quiz;
www.thesaddleranch.com

Yes, there's a stage with live fiddlers here, but let's be honest – the show at this Wild West-themed joint is less about the music and more about the mechanical bull. That's right: the mechanical bull. (You may remember it being ridden suggestively by Miranda in an episode of *Sex and the City*.) It's kitsch and it's crude, but the unique blend of hilarity and horror at watching Sunset Strip's party crowd try to channel their inner cowboy is worth the price of the steak alone.

» Don't leave without publicly embarrassing yourself on the mechanical bull. This ritual costs about $20 for two rounds – if you can hang on that long.

BLACK RABBIT ROSE
Map 3; 1719 N. Hudson Avenue, Hollywood; ///beyond.move.notice;
www.blackrabbitrose.com

Couldn't score an invite to the Magic Castle *(p137)*? Get your sleight-of-hand fix at Black Rabbit Rose. Run by immersive nightlife wizards the Houston brothers (see also Good Times at Davey Wayne's, *p65*), this Victorian-themed lounge feels brimming with secrets from the moment you step among its red velvet drapes. Bartenders conjure up mysterious drinks like the Dark Arts, while a trio of magical artists perform miraculous illusions for well-dressed dates and captivated groups of friends. Prepare to pick a card and have your mind blown.

Comedy Nights

L.A. is the historic home of ha ha, and there's no shortage of places to watch the pros whip up some laughs. For locals, a comedy show is the top go-to for an easy night out.

UCB THEATRE

Map 2; 5919 Franklin Avenue, Hollywood; ///await.fault.agree; www.ucbtheatre.com

Want to know who the next comedy superstar will be? Grab a ticket to a show at the UCB Theatre. It's the performance space for the UCB (Upright Citizens Brigade) comedy school, which is famed as a training ground for the next generation of alternative-skewing funny folk. The school's founders include Amy Poehler and *Veep*

Try it!
TV TAPING

Join the audience for a live TV taping of *Jimmy Kimmel Live* (El Capitan Theater) or *The Late Late Show* (CBS Studios). Tickets for both can be booked via 1iota *(https://1iota.com)*.

alum Matt Walsh, while Donald Glover and Aubrey Plaza are among those on the impressive alumni list; catch the latest class of improv and sketch students before they graduate to Hollywood.

FLAPPERS

Map 6; 102 E. Magnolia Boulevard, Burbank; ///march.bolt.crab; www.flapperscomedy.com

If you like eating as much as you like laughing, head to Flappers: comedy shows here come with dinner, too (note there's a minimum spend). The level of talent varies wildly – several weekly open mics showcase aspiring acts, while weekend shows typically boast bigger names – but you'll be howling with choke-on-your-food laughter no matter who you see.

THE COMEDY STORE

Map 3; 8433 Sunset Boulevard; West Hollywood; ///fire.exile.judge; www.thecomedystore.com

As much a staple of the raucous Sunset Strip as the nearby rock clubs, The Comedy Store has been on the map ever since Mitzi Shore – legendary comedy impresario and mother to performer Pauly Shore – steered it to success in the 1970s. Any and every comedian worth their salt has performed on the main stage or in the more intimate Belly Room – just check out the legions of A-listers' signatures on the outside of the venue for proof.

» **Don't leave without** staying to the bitter end of the show – big-name surprise guests are known to drop in at any point.

LAUGH FACTORY

Map 3; 8001 Sunset Boulevard, West Hollywood; ///helps.roses.mint;
www.laughfactory.com

Never has a venue's name been quite so on point. The Laugh
Factory's lineup is a rotating conveyor belt of household-name
stand-ups, whose top-of-the-range performances provoke huge
quantities of gasping-for-air laughter.

CHATTERBOX COMEDY

Map 6; 943 N. Citrus Avenue, Covina; ///agrees.families.terminal;
(626) 331-7500

Every Sunday, a quirky audience who prefer their comedy to be
less mainstream and more wild venture out to this welcoming
dive bar in the suburbs of San Gabriel Valley. And they're never
disappointed. The lineups of unknowns are where you're sure to
find your next favorite performer.

THE GROUNDLINGS THEATRE

Map 3; 7307 Melrose Avenue, West Hollywood; ///retire.occupy.fires;
www.groundlings.com

Will Ferrell. Melissa McCarthy. Maya Rudolph. Kristen Wiig. The list of
performers who got their start at this seminal venue reads like a who's
who of comedy A-listers. Weekend shows with the main company draw
the crowds, but any night here will have you in stitches.

» **Don't leave without** pausing to pay tribute at the plaque to The
Groundlings' founder and original director, Gary Austin.

Liked by the locals

"If you're looking for a witty evening, you have to stop by The Groundlings Theatre on Melrose. With improv and sketch shows happening weekly, this theater is a Hollywood staple."

CARRIE LAFERLE GERGELY,
MANAGING DIRECTOR OF THE GROUNDLINGS

Music Venues

From hair metal to folk rock to gangster rap, L.A.'s neighborhood venues have been the birthplace of generations of popular music. Catch local bands and touring acts at the city's best live music spots.

RESIDENT

Map 1; 428 S. Hewitt Street, Arts District; ///span.sock.knee; www.residentdtla.com

Resident feels more like a festival space than a concert venue, so do the sensible thing and make a gig here an all-day event. Rock up in the afternoon for a drink in the beer garden, grab dinner from one of the rotating food trucks, then head inside for a blast of whatever genre-pushing act is playing that night (it can be anything from psych to soul to hip-hop). Finish with a cozy cocktail next to the firepits.

THE SARDINE

Map 5; 1101 S. Pacific Avenue, San Pedro; ///carb.petition.towards; www.thesardinepedro.com

Get your best pogo moves ready for a night of punk rock at this combined venue, record store, and neighborhood bar. Small, hot, and fantastically loud, it's packed with South Bay residents of all

You can buy some vinyl or grab a beer on the patio any time The Sardine's open – not just during a show.

ages rocking out to noisy bands. If you're not dripping with sweat by the time the show's over, we'll be extremely disappointed.

WALT DISNEY CONCERT HALL
Map 1; 111 S. Grand Avenue, Downtown; ///loaf.funny.goals; www.laphil.com

Think classical music is stuffy? The Walt Disney Concert Hall is here to change your mind. Okay, it still offers plenty of Mozart and Beethoven, but you'll also find experimental modern works and fun holiday-themed shows. Our favorite event is the Casual Friday concert series – it includes a free (yes, free) post-show beer tasting with members of the orchestra.

» **Don't leave without** checking out the Blue Ribbon Garden, a hidden rooftop oasis dedicated to Lillian Disney.

THE ECHO + ECHOPLEX
Map 1; 1822 W. Sunset Boulevard, Echo Park; ///saying.firm.hype; www.theecho.com

This is, in fact, not one venue but two: The Echo, a dance floor-size bar on the street level, and Echoplex, an underground nightclub below. Every night brings a different crowd to both, depending on which reggae/dub DJ or indie band is playing. It's good to grab a ticket in advance, even if the scenester, go-with-the-flow Echo Park crowd gives off the vibe of not being the type to plan things in advance.

TROUBADOUR

Map 3; 9081 N. Santa Monica Boulevard, West Hollywood;
///nodded.humans.avoid; www.troubadour.com

If you're on the hunt for a slice of the city's music history, head to this iconic venue. Both Elton John and Guns N' Roses were catapulted to superstardom from here, and it's still the best place in town to check out up-and-coming talent. As you wait for the music to start, follow in the footsteps of Don Henley and Glenn Frey and grab a drink at the front bar – that's how the pair met in 1970, before going on to make music legend as the Eagles.

HOLLYWOOD BOWL

Map 3; 2301 N. Highland Avenue, Hollywood Hills; ///sing.fats.reward;
www.hollywoodbowl.com

Come summer, the Hollywood Bowl is *the* date venue for the city's desperate-to-impress romantics. A classical performance from the L.A. Philharmonic, a show by a big-name pop artist, or a celebration of Hollywood's iconic soundtracks – the music may change nightly, but the magic of a concert under the stars is always the same.

THE SMELL

Map 1; 247 S. Main Street, Downtown; ///fruit.forest.tower;
www.thesmell.org

The Smell has got all the grunge you'd expect of a DIY punk and experimental venue (back-alley entrance, graffitied walls), but with the unforeseen twist of a booze-free, all-ages door policy. This is the sort of place where you enter the underground music scene as a curious teen, and return as a jaded adult to blow off steam with a night of thrashing to loud, messy tunes.

THE ROXY

Map 3; 9009 Sunset Boulevard, West Hollywood;
///sushi.became.assume; www.theroxy.com

The legendary Sunset Strip might not be quite the incubator of arena-ready talent it once was, but the intimate Roxy is still doing the neighborhood's musical legacy proud. On any given night, an eclectic mix of locals can be found swaying to the melodies of singer-songwriters, bouncing around to hip-hop beats, or nodding energetically to the sounds of indie rock.

» Don't leave without visiting some of the Strip's other famous venues, including Whisky a Go Go and the Viper Room.

Thousands of Angelenos go to the movie screenings at Hollywood Forever Cemetery *(p125)*, but only a select group of music fans nab tickets to gigs at the cemetery's Masonic Lodge *(https://hollywoodforever. com)*. This atmospheric hall is about as cozy and intimate as venues get, with a wooden-beamed ceiling, candelabra lights, and only 150 tickets available per show. Think stripped-back, bare-your-soul sets from a mix of indie artists standing only yards away.

LGBTQ+ Scene

West Hollywood might be the center of LGBTQ+ life for many Angelenos, but the entire city has vibrant pockets that revel in queer culture, with nonstop dancing, loud music, and late nights.

HAMBURGER MARY'S

Map 5; 330 Pine Avenue, Long Beach; ///discount.lamp.backup; www.hamburgermarys.com

Hamburger might be in the name, but really people pack this place for everything but the food. The flamboyant bar and nightclub is front and center of Long Beach's gay scene, drawing a fun-loving crowd with some of the country's best-loved drag acts. Arrive early to get a great seat, bring plenty of dollar bills for tipping the performers, and be sure to order the orange creamsicle cocktail.

THE ABBEY

Map 3; 692 N. Robertson Boulevard, West Hollywood; ///glad.cliff.lonely; www.theabbeyweho.com

You wouldn't know it listening to the thumping pop music beats or watching the thrusting dancers on stage, but The Abbey started out as a modest coffee shop. It was opened in 1991, in the midst of the

AIDS crisis, as a safe space for gay men to be themselves and find a sense of community. And boy did it prove popular: The Abbey has since expanded five times (it's now the largest gay bar in WeHo) and is treasured as the heart of the area's LGBTQ+ scene.

HI TOPS

Map 3; 8933 Santa Monica Boulevard, West Hollywood;
///output.laser.fears; www.hitopsbar.com

With its cheeky name and locker-room aesthetic, this friendly WeHo sports bar is a laid-back spot to watch the game on a Sunday. Cheer on L.A.'s beloved Rams while sipping zingy cocktails and snacking on surprisingly good bar food (try the grilled cauliflower on a stick). Whose house? Rams' house!

» Don't leave without staying for happy hour – it's one of the best in West Hollywood, with $5 beers and bubbly.

CATCH ONE

Map 4; 4067 W. Pico Boulevard, Arlington Heights; ///foster.sofa.costs;
www.catch.one

Catch One is an L.A. institution. Founded back in 1973 by Jewel Thais-Williams, it was one of the first Black-owned discos in the country. Known then as Jewel's Catch One, the club essentially pioneered L.A.'s Black LGBTQ+ scene and became a legend of city nightlife (there's even a whole Netflix documentary about the place). Jewel herself is no longer running the joint (hence the current name), but her inclusive spirit lives on.

PRECINCT

Map 1; 357 S. Broadway, Downtown; ///enhancement.feed.colleague;
www.precinctdtla.com

Downtown finally has a massive, multiroom, party-focused gay club to rival the ones in WeHo: Precinct. Expect a trendy industrial aesthetic, cheap drinks, and a relaxed crowd where everyone just wants to blow off some steam.

AKBAR

Map 2; 4356 W. Sunset Boulevard, Silver Lake; ///sadly.cabin.fills;
www.akbarsilverlake.com

Gyrating gogo dancers not your thing? Bypass West Hollywood and hit up this unpretentious spot in Silver Lake. Eastsiders adore Akbar for its intimate, neighborhood vibe, with a crowd that's always welcoming and a dance floor that's always jumping to an epic mix of tunes.

» Don't leave without wandering into the back room to select some tunes on the beloved jukebox.

QUE SERA

Map 5; 1923 E. 7th Street, Long Beach; ///full.skip.bribing;
www.queseralb.wixsite.com/queseralb

Run by a team of gruff-but-kind lesbians, this divey bar is all about live shows: mainly music (singer Melissa Ethridge got her start here), but also comedy and a bit of burlesque. It's dark, loud, and just how the regulars like it — especially when it comes to the heavy-handed pours at the bar.

Liked by the locals

"Precinct is special because it's a space in L.A. gay culture where all types of queer people can fit in and feel at ease. It also happens to be the best place for drag queen sightings. I once saw Trixie Mattel and Jackie Beat in one weekend."

REBECCA KRAMER,
EXECUTIVE ASSISTANT

Cool Clubs

Ready to shake it to cumbia, EDM, or hip-hop?
L.A.'s expansive club scene has you covered.
Whatever your jam, you'll find a spot to
strut your stuff.

PANAMERICAN NIGHT CLUB

Map 1; 2601 W. Temple Street, Westlake; ///assets.enhancement.focus;
www.panamericannightclub.com

If you're looking to party to some Latin beats, Panamerican is
the place to be. Every day here brings a different sound – there's
parranda on Wednesdays, tropical night on Fridays, and rumba
on Sundays, plus countless other genres on the days in between.
Come dressed to the nines and ready to show off your moves.

SHORT STOP

Map 1; 1455 W. Sunset Boulevard, Echo Park; ///alone.oiled.tigers;
www.instagram.com/theshortstopechopark

By day, this neighborhood dive bar is a pregame staple for
baseball fans heading to nearby Dodger Stadium (hence the
name). By night, however, it morphs into a pumping dance
destination filled with Echo Park hipsters out for a good time.

The music changes daily, but some things are guaranteed: cheap drinks, a nonjudgmental crowd, and almost certainly at least one person on the dance floor in a Dodgers cap.

LA CITA

Map 1; 336 S. Hill Street, Downtown; ///cool.punk.influencing; www.lacitabar.com

We don't like to brag, but La Cita has twice appeared in *Esquire* magazine's "Best Bars in America" feature. Not to say that means you'll get high-end gloss here: this place is classic dive bar, complete with all the sweat and red neon lights that entails. It's the fun atmosphere and live music that make it special, with a lineup of cumbia legends, local bands, and DJs loved by everyone from abuelos in cowboy hats to excitable 20-somethings.

» Don't leave without taking a breather in El Patio at the back, an airy outdoor space that has a more low-key DJ vibe to the one inside.

It's generally accepted that hitting a club in L.A. requires putting on your most expensive clothes and doing your best to impress everyone you encounter. Not so at Bootie L.A. *(https://bootiemashup.com)*, a scene-y but still surprisingly low-key club night that rotates through a few key spots. You can count on eclectic mash-ups featuring unlikely pairings of pop, rock, and rap, enjoyed by a crowd of irony-loving locals.

EXCHANGE LA

Map 1; 618 S. Spring Street, Downtown; ///dame.brave.glad;
https://exchangela.com

If you've always wanted to re-create Coachella's famed Sahara
tent – full of fashionable, care-free people in the biggest dance
frenzy imaginable – this massive club in Downtown is for you.
Spread over four stories in the former L.A. Stock Exchange building,
it's packed with party-focused clubbers and EDM fans of all stripes
losing themselves wildly to the music.

ZEBULON

Map 2; 2478 Fletcher Drive, Frogtown; ///origin.online.hours;
https://zebulon.la

For East Coast transplants seeking out Big Apple vibes, Zebulon
quickly cures any homesickness – once based in hipster-central
Williamsburg, it's found a new home in similarly trendy Frogtown.
Industrial-style decor? Check. On-trend DJs and theme nights?
Check. A too-cool-to-care crowd casually letting their hair down?
Double check. Who needs rainy old New York, anyway?

SKYBAR

Map 3; 8440 Sunset Boulevard, West Hollywood; ///tiles.saving.locals;
www.sbe.com

Come prepared to give off your most nonchalant, over-it L.A. vibe
imaginable. This glitzy rooftop destination on Sunset Boulevard
comes with a high-glam atmosphere soundtracked by a mix of rap

Come dressed to impress: the bouncers favor the top-tier guests and are known to be unforgiving.

and house music. It's the haunt of the rich, young, and extremely well-connected, and if you're in the mood for bottle service, you can't do much better.

AVALON HOLLYWOOD

Map 3; 1735 Vine Street, Hollywood; ///crown.intent.nuns;
https://avalonhollywood.com

Tinseltown is constantly reinventing itself, and the Avalon is no exception. Having hosted Lucille Ball's radio show, The Beatles' first West Coast appearance, and The Ramones' final concert, this historic venue found new life in the 2000s as one of L.A.'s best superclubs. Expect high-profile DJs, a sound system that'll leave your ears buzzing, and a gleeful, dance-like-nobody's-watching energy that keeps going all night.

» Don't leave without seeing if you can guess the spot in the main theater where a pre-presidential Richard Nixon gave his famous "Checkers speech" back in 1952.

CIRCLE BAR

Map 4; 2926 Main Street, Santa Monica; ///scarcely.exist.never;
www.circle-bar.com

As night falls, groups of energetic Santa Monica beachgoers leave the sand behind and congregate at Circle Bar to continue the party. Hip-hop tracks bring the beats, while punchy drinks keep the club's laid-back revelers pulsating on the dance floor.

Late-Night Bites

Anyone who says nothing good happens after dark hasn't explored the after-hours food scene in L.A. Here, you can party all night and still nosh on whatever you desire – base layer of alcohol entirely optional.

LEO'S TACOS

Map 4; 1515 S. La Brea Avenue, Mid City; ///stole.asks.tested;
www.leostacostruck.com

If you're ever hungry after dark in L.A., keep your eyes out for a string of patio lights, a makeshift tent or food truck, and, if you're lucky, a spinning trompo of meat. These pop-up taquerias are a staple of the city's late-night food scene and attract hungry revelers like moths to a flame. It's almost impossible to pick a favorite, but, if

Try it!
GO ON A TACO HUNT

Drive south out of downtown L.A. on any Friday or Saturday night, and for the next 100 blocks you'll find countless streetside taco stalls. Those near the tire shops on South Alameda are always a good place to start.

pushed, we'd have to go for Leo's Tacos. It's got a fleet of seven trucks across the city, so you're always sure to find one nearby; this one on La Brea holds a special place in our heart for being the first.

» Don't leave without trying *tacos al pastor*: freshly sliced meat from the spit, served in a palm-size tortilla with a piece of pineapple.

PINK'S HOT DOGS

Map 3; 709 N. La Brea Avenue, Hollywood; ///sadly.logic.influencing; www.pinkshollywood.com

The long lines, the bean-free chili, the satisfying snap of the most famous hot dog in L.A. between your teeth. Yes, Pink's is one hyped-up Hollywood staple that is definitely worth the wait (its mustardy Polish dog in particular is a rare find in the L.A. food scene). By day, the stand is crammed with frazzled families and tourists, but come weekend nights, it's taken over by a cheerful crowd of tipsy industry folks and club-bound crews, fueling up until a cool 1a.m.

MEL'S DRIVE-IN

Map 3; 8585 Sunset Boulevard, West Hollywood; ///owners.jumped.news; www.melsdrive-in.com

Don't let the name fool you: none of L.A.'s four Mel's Drive-In locations will actually serve you food in your cars. Even so, with classic diner dishes cooked in historic Googie structures – think neon signs and tableside jukeboxes – Mel's is still the all-night diner of 1950s teenage dreams. Hit up this branch in West Hollywood after a night of raucous partying on Sunset Strip.

RUEN PAIR

Map 2; 5257 Hollywood Boulevard, Thai Town; ///milk.bind.modes; www.ruenpairthai.com

The food at this strip-mall Thai restaurant is good (it's got all the usual spicy standards and fragrant classics), but that's not why we love it. No, the reason we keep stumbling in here after closing time is because it has no set operating hours – meaning that if it's busy, it stays open, often as late as 3a.m. on weekends.

YANGJI GAMJATANG

Map 2; 3470 W. 6th Street, Koreatown; ///energy.float.erase; (323) 827-8450

We've all been there: glassy-eyed at the end of an evening out, with a stomach begging for something warm and nourishing to soak up the night's sins. If you're anywhere near Koreatown the next time this happens, your tomorrow-morning self will thank you for seeking out Yangji Gamjatang. This low-key spot specializes in the namesake Korean pork stew, which comes to the table in a bubbling hot pot, red and hulking with steaming bones. It's hangover cure heaven.

CANTER'S

Map 3; 419 N. Fairfax Avenue, Fairfax; ///oddly.gangs.mental; www.cantersdeli.com

Once upon a time, L.A. used to have dozens of Jewish delis serving towering meaty sandwiches. Although many have now disappeared, Canter's remains a stalwart of the deli-diner experience – complete

with an attached dive bar, 24-hour service, and a multipage menu
that goes as wide as it does deep. All walks of life swarm to this
iconic destination during the small hours, reviving with classic
comfort food like corned beef, brisket, and matzo ball soup.

» Don't leave without stopping by the pastry counter on your way
out and buying some cakes, pastries, or sweets to go.

FORMOSA CAFE

Map 3; 7156 Santa Monica Boulevard, West Hollywood;
///actual.indoor.enter; www.theformosacafe.com

Fancy ending your night with a touch of Old Hollywood glamour?
Head to the Formosa. It was once an after-hours favorite of the likes
of Frank Sinatra, Ava Gardner, and Elvis Presley. The moody lighting
provides protective cover for bleary eyes, while the famous chow fun
noodles bring salvation to your stomach.

Yes, In-N-Out *(www.in-n-out.
com)* is a chain, but it's our
chain and we say its burgers
are some of the best late-night
fast food around. The trick, as
all Angelenos know, is to learn
the lingo so you can order from
the secret menu. Try a Flying
Dutchman (two slices of cheese
between two burger patties), a
Scooby snack (patty, no bun),
grilled cheese (no patty), or a
wish burger (salad-only veggie
option). And always order the
animal fries (with signature
sauce, cheese, and onions).

Whisky a Go Go
*has been a rock 'n' roll
Sunset Strip staple since
1964. Famously, it once
had The Doors as its
house band.*

Close out the night
BARNEY'S BEANER
This L.A. staple isn't the mo
refined, but after a night of high jin
a relaxed watering hole with tal
games is maybe just what you nee

WEST   SUNSET   BOULEVARD

HOLLOWAY   DRIVE

PALM AVENUE

SANTA MONICA BOULEVARD

WEST
HOLLYWOOD

NORTH LA CIENEGA BOULEVARD

Dance with abandon at
ROCCO'S
Located along the buzzy stretch
of Santa Monica Boulevard
(known colloquially as Boys Town),
this raucous gay club is co-owned
by *NSYNC's Lance Bass.

NORTH SAN VICENTE BLVD

HUNTLEY DRIVE

Raise a glass at
PUMP
Yes, TV tourists love this garden bar,
owned by *The Real Housewives of
Beverly Hills* star Lisa Vanderpump.
But it's an essential stop on nights
out, especially with LGBTQ+ folk.

MELROSE   AVENUE

Enjoy the scenery at
CATCH LA
There's no better place to see and
be seen than at this rooftop bar and
restaurant. Indulge in a cocktail and
seafood with a view, and keep your eyes
peeled for celebrities doing the same
(reservations are a must).

A night out in
West Hollywood

Mobster Bugsy Siegel lived at what's today **Tower Bar**, *in the Sunset Tower Hotel. John Wayne and Frank Sinatra also called the building home.*

The folk of West Hollywood (or WeHo) have long been a rebellious bunch. In the 1920s, rather than have their patch incorporated into the City of Los Angeles, locals opted to remain under the jurisdiction of L.A. County. Gambling was illegal in the city, you see, so casinos and nightclubs thrived here, especially along Sunset Boulevard. WeHo residents still love a good time, spending their evenings partying at scene-y bars, swinging LGBTQ+ nightclubs, and welcoming dives.

1. Catch LA
8715 Melrose Avenue;
www.catchrestaurants.com
///forks.hurt.agree

2. Pump
8948 Santa Monica
Boulevard; www.
pumprestaurant.com
///tuck.park.agents

3. Rocco's
8900 Santa Monica
Boulevard;
www.roccosweho.com
///codes.roses.return

4. Barney's Beanery
8447 Santa Monica
Boulevard; https://
barneysbeanery.com
///shout.clown.ocean

 **Tower Bar** ///stocks.total.valve

Whisky a Go Go
///lobby.blitz.basis

MELROSE AVENUE

BEVERLY
GROVE

ULEVARD

OUTDOORS

Surf, sand, and almost year-round sun – outdoor living is what L.A.'s all about. Whether they're lazing on the beach or hiking in the hills, Angelenos are always found outside.

Beautiful Beaches

You can't come to L.A. and not dip your toes in the ocean. Everyone knows about the famous beaches of Venice and Santa Monica, but here's where the locals go when they want to avoid the crowds.

PENINSULA BAYSIDE BEACH

Map 5; E. Bayshore Walk between 55th Place and 68th Place, Long Beach; ///desktop.strict.material

Looking for a quiet spot to chill with a good book? Head east on Ocean Boulevard until you hit The Peninsula. This thin strip of land is barely two blocks wide, with upscale houses down the center and tranquil sandy beaches on either side. You can lay your towel out anywhere, but those in the know go for the northern coast, facing

Try it!
GO FOR A PADDLE

If you're feeling energetic, Bayside Beach is a great place from which to go kayaking or paddleboarding for a few hours. Rentals are available year-round near Bayshore Park, at the start of The Peninsula.

Alamitos Bay (hence, Bayside Beach). That way, you can while away the hours without getting sand blown in your paperback by the afternoon winds that whip the Pacific side.

BURNOUT BEACH

Map 5; 1801 Esplanade, Redondo Beach; ///cage.drives.newly

Locals can't agree how this surfer's haven got its name (some say it's a reference to a historic fire, others a nod to the bonfire parties held here), but we can guarantee it's not an indictment of the caliber of people who frequent it. Here, you'll encounter L.A. beach life at its laid-back best: swimmers and surfers bobbing in the waves, couples strolling hand in hand, and groups of friends just chilling in the sun.

BRUCE'S BEACH

Map 4; 2600 Highland Avenue, Manhattan Beach; ///wakes.normal.amuse

You won't just find sand at Bruce's Beach, you'll uncover some important history, too. In the early 1900s, ambitious couple Willa and Charles Bruce established a thriving seaside resort here for Manhattan Beach's Black community. Within a few decades, however, white residents had run the business out of town and local government seized the land for a park. Ownership of the property was finally returned to the Bruce family in 2021; for now, it remains a peaceful spot to ponder the past while overlooking the ocean.

» Don't leave without pausing to read the plaque in the middle of the park that tells the Bruces' story.

LEO CARRILLO STATE PARK

Map 6; 35000 Pacific Coast Highway, Malibu; ///fuss.chemicals.irritant

Want to enjoy a beach day with your four-legged partner-in-crime?
Then you'll love this serene stretch of sand. As one of the few beaches
in Los Angeles that welcomes dogs (they just have to be on a leash,
and you'll need to stay between lifeguard towers three and four), it
draws pets and their owners from all over.

ZUMA BEACH

**Map 6; 30000 Pacific Coast Highway, Malibu;
///transcript.avert.mavericks; https://beaches.lacounty.gov/zuma-beach**

Cruise up the Pacific Coast Highway, past the moneyed mansions
of Malibu, and keep going until you're almost at the Ventura
County line. There you'll find the cleanest (and coldest) 2 miles
(3 km) of ocean water in L.A. Zuma Beach is long, wide, and comes
with big waves that are perfect for board sports. If you want to get
a taste of California surf culture, this is the place to post up.

SOUTH BEACH SANTA MONICA

Map 4; 3400 Barnard Way, Santa Monica; ///limit.client.robot

We get it – you want to see if Santa Monica and Venice live up
to the hype. Well (spoiler alert), they do, but they're pretty much
always packed with people. So once you're done checking out the
boardwalk and pier, stake out a space for the rest of the day on this
stretch of sand and parkland between the two. Comparatively free
of tourists, it draws a low-key crowd of runners out on their daily jog,

Hit up Main Street in Santa Monica for the best bars and shops on the south side of the 10 Freeway.

families hitting the seaside playground, and kids from across L.A. riding bikes down the historic beach path. It's a relative haven of calm amid the chaos.

OCEAN TRAILS RESERVE

Map 5; 1 Trump National Drive, Rancho Palos Verdes;
///lifelike.drillers.wayward; https://rpvca.gov/1154/Ocean-Trails-Reserve

Sometimes, when you've had a bad week, all you want to do is escape the city and lose yourself in nature. At these moments, the Ocean Trails Reserve is the perfect tonic. Part rolling hills pocked with fancy mansions and part network of protected lands, it's laced with paths along breathtaking bluffs. Hike down the cliffs and surround yourself with native sea life and soothing ocean views. By the time high tide washes you back out and up to your car, you'll feel as good as new.

>> Don't leave without grabbing a sandwich for lunch at Busy Bee, on your way through nearby San Pedro.

DOCKWEILER STATE BEACH

Map 4; 12000 Vista del Mar, Playa del Rey; ///flame.spits.gloves;
https://beaches.lacounty.gov/dockweiler-beach

Behind you is a power plant and overhead are the planes taking off from LAX – but in front of you lies glorious open sea, with miles of sandy beach stretching out to either side. It's about as real as the beach in L.A. gets, and everyone who comes here to roast marshmallows on the bonfire pits knows it.

Green Spaces

Sure, San Francisco has Golden Gate Park, but L.A.'s gone one better with large, grassy expanses in every part of town. Park culture here is all about relaxing – enjoying some greenery while soaking up the sun.

ERNEST E. DEBS PARK

Map 6; 4235 Monterey Road, Montecito Hills; ///little.react.pets; www.laparks.org

Debs Park is the ultimate symbol of L.A.'s community spirit and love of the outdoors. It's the hiking groups that meet weekly to trek through the natural arroyo woodlands – among the last in Southern California. It's the families who gather at the picnic sites to catch up while the kids play and birds flit overhead. And it's the volunteers who inspire locals to care for the natural world at the Audubon Center (in the U.S.'s first carbon-neutral building, no less).

ECHO PARK LAKE

Map 1; 751 Echo Park Avenue, Echo Park; ///fees.dare.almost

This centerpiece of the Echo Park neighborhood is one of L.A.'s original builds, dating back to 1860. It's been a hub for residents ever since, where impressive views of the Downtown skyline backdrop lush

Get out on the lake in one of the swan-shaped pedal boats – it's a fun way to enjoy the water.

strolls along the water. Pass the day here reading on the grass and tucking into *elotes* (corn) and *paletas* (popsicles) from roaming street food vendors.

GRAND PARK

Map 1; 200 N. Grand Avenue, Downtown; ///dined.lasted.cans; www.grandparkla.org

In the shadow of City Hall, this strip of grass prides itself on being "the park for everyone." It's a microcosm of L.A.'s people and their interests – a public square to come together for protests, concerts, and an annual New Year's Eve light display. Events aside, it's simply a much-needed bit of greenery where office workers hang on their lunch break, children splash in the fountain, and visiting couples look to re-create the romantic moments filmed here for *Pretty Woman*.

GRIFFITH PARK

Map 2; 4730 Crystal Springs Drive, Los Feliz; ///pies.leave.skill; www.laparks.org

Angelenos are quick to boast that Griffith Park is five times the size of N.Y.C.'s famed Central Park. And, as the largest park in L.A., it tends to be every local's favorite green space. Pretty much all walks of life are found here, from the Los Feliz hipsters on their look-at-me morning cardio sessions, to the families who hit up L.A. Zoo on the weekend.
» Don't leave without hiking to Amir's Garden, a serene oasis where flowers and jaw-dropping views of the city and mountains await.

Solo, Pair, Crowd

L.A. has plenty of places where you and your friends can get away from the concrete jungle.

FLYING SOLO
Beautiful blooms
Take some time out in Exposition Park and stop to (literally) smell the roses. From December to April, the Rose Garden here blooms with approximately 16,000 flowers, creating a heavenly setting for indulging in a bit of me-time.

IN A PAIR
Gossip and greenery
With its lush foliage, peaceful paths, and pretty water features, Los Angeles County Arboretum is a cute spot to meet up with a pal. Find a bench in a shady nook and catch up on all the latest gossip.

FOR A CROWD
Fun among the flowers
Gather the gang to play hide-and-seek at the South Coast Botanic Garden. Eight sculptures have been hidden among the foliage, and guests of all ages are encouraged to go and hunt for them.

DESCANSO GARDENS

Map 6; 1418 Descanso Drive, La Cañada Flintridge; ///ranch.text.life;
www.descansogardens.org

A love for plants has always been at the heart of Descanso, from its early days as a private garden to its 1950 adoption as a public space. It remains a place for nature-loving folk, to wander through oak forests or breathe in the aroma of fruit trees. Heavenly.

HUNTINGTON LIBRARY

Map 6; 1151 Oxford Road, San Marino; ///note.going.awake;
www.huntington.org

The former estate of railroad magnate Henry Huntington is now a museum, but many locals bypass the interior for an amble around the gardens. And why not? There are lots of lush themed areas, including a desert garden and a Japanese garden, to name just a couple.

» Don't leave without checking out the museum. It's got a collection of notable artwork, plus an original copy of the Gutenberg Bible.

ELYSIAN PARK

Map 1; 929 Academy Road, Elysian Park; ///plan.brains.priced;
www.laparks.org

Angelenos are passionate about the Dodgers, so it's no surprise that they love this park, too – it's home to Dodger Stadium. On game days, you'll find the grass covered in high-spirited baseball fans; the rest of the time, it's sprinkled with joggers, hikers, and cyclists, enjoying views of the city as they hit the trails.

Heavenly Hikes

They say Angelenos never walk anywhere, but we're here to tell you different. Come the weekend, locals swap the concrete jungle for the dirt trails and fresh air of the city's beautiful public nature reserves.

RUNYON CANYON

Map 3; start at 2000 N. Fuller Avenue, Hollywood Hills; ///diner.flats.steer

This isn't one for lacing up your muddy boots: Runyon Canyon is all about seeing and being seen. That means donning your best yoga pants and designer sneakers for the 2.7-mile (4.3-km) loop, along which you're likely to spot a celebrity or two walking their pooch. Once you reach the top, though, you won't care a jot about the up-and-coming actor you might have seen along the way – it's the pools and houses dotting the Hollywood hills that will have your full attention.

CHANTRY FLAT

Map 6; Chantry Flat Road, Arcadia; ///fully.goatskin.buffets

Chantry Flat has a lot going for it. First off, it's home to the last donkey-packing station in the San Gabriel Mountains, reminiscent of a time when freight was transported via pack animal. Secondly, it's the trailhead for the rugged but beautiful Gabrielino Trail, which

Get there early. The parking lot fills up fast, so if you're late, you'll have to park lower down and hike up.

winds past century-old settler cabins on the way to Mt. Wilson. The 15-mile (24-km) hike to the summit is a killer, but the views throughout are totally worth it.

CULVER CITY STAIRS

Map 4; start at Jefferson Boulevard, Culver City; ///spout.poker.fortunate

Stairs might not ordinarily scream "hike," but this outdoor staircase is notorious for being quite the workout. Also known as the Baldwin Hills Scenic Overlook, it's always bustling with L.A. fitness fanatics getting their cardio in, either running or power-walking up the 282 uneven steps to the top. Shaky knees are guaranteed by the end, so take a moment of rest and soak up the amazing views of L.A. below.

» Don't leave without walking to downtown Culver City after to reward yourself with brunch – you'll need the carbs, right?

MURPHY RANCH

Map 6; start S. on Sullivan Fire Road, Pacific Palisades; ///guitar.vision.fully

L.A. hikes aren't all sweeping views of glam penthouses – take this 3.8-mile (6.1-km) loop, for example. In the prelude to World War II, Nazi sympathizers set up a hideout in this canyon as they awaited the fall of the U.S. to the Third Reich. No such victory came, of course, and the camp was eventually raided and shut down by authorities. Since then, the steep descent into the 1930s town has become a beacon for intrepid explorers, who come to snap the collapsing graffiti-laden leftovers.

MT. LOWE/ECHO MOUNTAIN

Map 6; start W. on Mt. Lowe Road, Altadena; ///misty.hike.casino

Many parts of L.A. are synonymous with luxury, and while the same can't be said for this arduous hike, the echoes of an opulent past are there to see. Back in the Victorian era, a sprawling hotel sat at the top of Mt. Lowe; to get there, wealthy denizens would take a train up the steep 2.5-mile (4-km) trail, ready to party. Ill-timed fires and floods damaged the facilities, but remnants of the site – an old cog wheel, the estate's foundation – offer a pretty cool insight into an L.A. of the past.

LOS LIONES

Map 6; start on 510 Los Liones Drive, Pacific Palisades; ///held.awake.active

It might be a short 3-mile (5-km) route, but you have to work hard on this grueling hike. There are plenty of brutal switchbacks (trails that cut suddenly from one direction to the next while ascending a sharp incline) and not a ton of shade, so pack plenty of water and sunscreen. A bench at the end of the trail offers respite for those

Shh!

If you want a cool desert vibe without going all the way to Joshua Tree, head just north of L.A. to Vasquez Rocks. It has a great selection of hiking trails and lots of stunning, otherworldly sandstone formations (so otherworldly, in fact, that they've appeared several times as a backdrop in *Star Trek*).

burning calves, while you soak up rad views of the Pacific. Little wonder the trail is loved by those seeking another reason to show off that they live in L.A. (as if they need one).

SOLSTICE CANYON

Map 6; start on Solstice Canyon Road, Malibu; ///abide.paddock.loners
You'll rarely hear locals complaining about the weather, but a bit of shade from the blazing sun is always welcome. This easy 3-mile (5-km) stroll through the former grounds of a Malibu estate offers just that, with shaded paths and streams and small pools to cool off in. It feels worlds away from the nearby packed beaches – though you'll still get a taste of the ocean with the awesome views.

» Don't leave without seeing the rare year-round waterfall at the back of the property.

BRIDGE TO NOWHERE

Map 6; start on Camp Bonita Road, Azusa; ///sponsoring.cuckoo.bonbons
In a city where everyone's got to be going somewhere, the Bridge to Nowhere might seem out of place. Seek out this incongruous structure on this 10.5-mile (17-km) hike in the San Gabriel Mountains. After the trek out to the East Fork of the San Gabriel River, you'll come across a fully built bridge that has no roads attaching it on either side. It's the eerie remnant of a road construction that started and stopped in the 1930s, until a severe flood stymied attempts for good. You can hike across the bridge or even bungee jump, but most locals take a relaxing dip in the swimming hole beneath it – a blessing on a hot day.

Movie Magic

Getting déjà vu while checking out L.A.? It's probably because you're somewhere that you've seen on screen. Industry icons are sprinkled all over town – these are our favorite, most easily accessible spots.

GRIFFITH OBSERVATORY

Map 2; 2800 East Observatory Road, Griffith Park; ///lime.liner.organs; https://griffithobservatory.org

As if the great views weren't enough of a reason to visit this storied observatory, it's also been a location for some of Hollywood's most memorable scenes. Come here to live out your best *La La Land* fantasy, or rail against the world like James Dean in *Rebel Without a Cause*. Just watch out for the dinosaurs (only kidding) – the building also played the welcome center in *Jurassic Park*.

CIRCUS LIQUOR

Map 6; 5600 Vineland Avenue, North Hollywood; ///heap.kicked.racing; https://circusliquor.gotoliquorstore.com

Remember that scene in *Clueless* where Cher gets mugged? Well, the parking lot outside this liquor store is where it happened. (You'll know you're in the right place when you spot the giant neon sign featuring a rather menacing clown.) Admittedly, it's not the most glamorous movie location we could have chosen, but it's a signature landmark of the Valley – and *Clueless* is a 90s icon of Valley life. So, like, whatever.

POINT DUME

Map 6; Westward Beach Road, Malibu; ///nicer.fuel.reroute

If you're a Marvel fan, you may recognize this rocky promontory as the location of Tony Stark's coastal mansion in the *Iron Man* movies. But that's not Point Dume's most famous cinematic cameo; it was also the setting for the pivotal final scene in the original *Planet of the Apes*. We won't spoil the ending for you, but let's just say it's nearly as startling as the views here.

» Don't leave without making an appointment to tour the nearby Melody Ranch Studio, where countless Westerns have been filmed.

BRADBURY BUILDING

**Map 1; 304 S. Broadway, Downtown; ///shop.result.shadow;
www.laconservancy.org/locations/bradbury-building**

Even if you don't know the Bradbury Building by name, it'll definitely look familiar when you step inside. The atrium of this National Historic Landmark – with its distinctive staircases and ironwork – has supplied the backdrop for everything from *Blade Runner* to *The Artist*, not to mention countless music videos. It's a working office building, but you're free to go inside and have a wander around the first floor – unless it's closed for filming, of course.

USC CAMPUS

Map 4; University Park Campus, University Park; ///react.cone.hills; www.usc.edu

If you've ever seen students hurrying to class on the big screen, chances are they were filmed at USC. Its lovely campus and central L.A. location make it a prime pick for college footage. It's even stood in for other real-life schools – like in Forrest Gump's graduation scene, where it filled in for the University of Alabama, and key moments from *Legally Blonde*, where it substituted for Harvard.

HOLLYWOOD SIGN

Map 2; 5600 Sunset Boulevard, Hollywood; ///handwriting.chairs.payer; www.hollywoodsign.org

Ah, the Hollywood sign. Nothing symbolizes the alluring promise of Tinseltown quite like this fabled landmark. There are plenty of well-known places to see it from, including Griffith Observatory *(p176)* and the Ovation Hollywood shopping center. Our pick, though, is the top floor of the parking structure at the Home Depot on Sunset Boulevard – it's (sort of) like your own private viewing deck.

HOLLYWOOD WALK OF FAME

Map 3; Hollywood Boulevard, Hollywood; ///legs.friday.strict; https://walkoffame.com

There's no denying it's supremely touristy, but you can't really say you've been to L.A. without a stroll along this star-studded sidewalk. It's most fun if you make a game of it: look for obscure celebrities you forgot existed, and discover which unfortunate people have been consigned to the second-tier streets off Hollywood Boulevard. Bonus points if you can spot the two Harrison Fords – the one you (probably) haven't heard of was a silent film star.

» **Don't leave without** finding your celebrity hand and foot double among the prints outside Grauman's Chinese Theatre.

WARNER BROS STUDIO TOUR

Map 6; 3400 Warner Boulevard, Burbank; ///extra.counts.trips; www.wbstudiotour.com

Don't have any Hollywood connections? Then your best option for visiting a studio lot is to take the guided tour at Warner Bros. Yes, you could do something similar at Universal Studios or Disneyland, but only here can you see the actual *Friends* fountain (and the Central Perk café), as well as the apartment sets from *The Big Bang Theory*. Oh, and did we mention there's also a Batmobile you can look inside? If you're super lucky, you might even spot some celebrities filming (it does happen, we promise you).

Try it!
PRETTY WOMAN

Have your own Julia Roberts moment by going (window) shopping on Rodeo Drive. If you've got the budget, you can even book a full "Pretty Woman for a Day" experience at the Beverly Wilshire hotel from the movie.

Scenic Road Trips

When the weekend finally arrives, Angelenos have
one thing in mind: a road trip. Make like a local
and hit the road in search of California's most
gorgeous spots and landscapes.

MULHOLLAND DRIVE

Map 3; start at Cahuenga Boulevard, Hollywood Hills; ///jaws.yarn.wire

Stuck in inner-city traffic? Fantasizing about a nonstop drive through the Hollywood Hills? Look no further than Mulholland Drive, a road so famous that David Lynch named a movie after it. The 21-mile (34-km) stretch runs east–west along the upper ridge of the mountains that separate the San Fernando Valley from L.A. proper. Aside from a glorious lack of traffic jams, you'll be rewarded with stunning vistas with every hairpin curve. Just take it slow, yeah?

OCEAN BOULEVARD

Map 5; start at Alamitos Beach, Long Beach; ///ruins.gives.pillows

At the southernmost end of L.A., on the Long Beach coast, the bike path parallel to Ocean Boulevard makes for an idyllic afternoon cycle. Channel your inner movie star by donning your sunglasses and pedal past the oceanfront condos and swaying palm trees that line

If you prefer four wheels to two, hop in your ride and drive the route along actual Ocean Boulevard.

this short, scenic route (it's just a few miles long). Continue east to Alamitos Park with extreme ocean views of sailboats, barges, and tropical-looking artificial islands.

PACIFIC COAST HIGHWAY

Map 6; start on Pacific Coast Highway, Santa Monica; ///guess.groom.plates
Picture a typical California road and you'll likely think of the Pacific Coast Highway, which traces the state's stunning coastline for 655 miles (1,005 km). Starting in L.A. as a series of urban boulevards, the highway is especially popular (read: busy) between Santa Monica and Malibu. And it's easy to see why: with mountains on one side and the Pacific Ocean on the other, cyclists and convertibles all slow to savor the salty air and ogle the beachfront mansions.
>> Don't leave without taking your bike and enjoying a detour just north of the Santa Monica Pier to Venice Beach. The views are epic.

PALOS VERDES DRIVE SOUTH

Map 5; start at Western Avenue and 25th Street, San Pedro; ///rounded.inspections.employer
Ah, the heavenly Palos Verdes Peninsula: rugged Californian cliffs, deep-blue surf, and ocean-view houses atop it all. The scenery is constantly changing, too, thanks to the battering wind and waves eroding the dramatic landscape. Line up a playlist ("California Dreamin'," anyone?) and join the road from San Pedro for unparalleled views of the Pacific, Catalina Island, and untouched beaches below.

PALMS TO PINES SCENIC BYWAY

Map 6; start on Highway 74, Palm Desert; ///toddler.probing.suspect

Families climb into their SUVs, picnics in tow, and leave the city for this truly unique scenic byway. The 67-mile (108-km) road transforms from a desert oasis (near Coachella Valley, no less) into snow-peaked mountains, providing ample landscapes to stop for a stretch of the legs and an alfresco lunch.

HIGHWAY 101

Map 6; start at Los Angeles Street entrance to Highway 101, Downtown; ///slides.lower.belly

Highway 101 connects downtown L.A. with San Francisco, but locals know they don't have to travel all the way to the Bay to get dreamy coastal views. About an hour outside of L.A., mountains spring up on the right, and sand and sea glitters on the left. A few small towns of hardy seaside homes later and Santa Barbara appears, with its stroll-worthy pier, historical Spanish mission, and lively downtown: just the ticket for a warm Saturday afternoon.

» Don't leave without spending some time in Santa Barbara's "Funk Zone," an artistic neighborhood full of independent stores.

ANGELES CREST HIGHWAY

Map 6; start on Highway 2, La Cañada-Flintridge; ///fast.stands.then

Of course L.A. locals love their city, but sometimes a change of scene is needed. Thankfully, the Angeles Crest Highway is on hand to sweep weary office workers and creatively blocked artists out into the wilderness. For 66 miles (106 km), the scenic byway twists and winds around picturesque peaks, hugging the rim of the San Gabriel Mountains as they blend into the San Bernardino range and snaking around the iconic Mount Wilson Observatory.

JOSHUA TREE NATIONAL PARK

Map 6; start on Interstate 10, Santa Monica; ///shuts.spike.kick

Americans are rightly proud of their national parks – their shared backyards – which span every kind of landscape imaginable. Angelenos' closest park is Joshua Tree, famed for its otherworldly yucca palms. We say "close"; it's a good 127-mile (205-km) drive from L.A., making this the perfect summer road trip with friends (hello, car pool). Once your pals have piled into the car, take the Interstate 10 east through the windy fields of giant turbines, and up onto Highway 62. Stay on the 62 until you reach the park entrance in the city of Joshua Tree. Here, you'll be greeted by incredible views of the Mojave and Sonoran deserts and, importantly, a number of restaurants for a hard-earned meal.

Try it!
STARGAZING

After concentrating on the road to get to Joshua Tree, look up to the night sky. Park up at one of the park's roadside pullouts or camp and sleep beneath the stars *(https://home.nps.gov/jotr/index.htm).*

VISTA DEL MAR

EL SEGUNDO

FREEWAY

DIEGO

ROSECRANS

SAN

Pick up your wheels at
MANHATTAN BEACH
E-BIKE RENTALS

E-bikes are all the rage in L.A. Hire yours for the day at this dedicated rental hub and get pedaling.

1

MANHATTAN
BEACH

Continue on to
BRUCE'S BEACH

Pause at the site of the West Coast's first Black-owned beach resort, which is now a hilltop park with views of the Strand below.

2

SOUTH BAY

Fuel up at
MANHATTAN BEACH PIER

Stop for lunch in the South Bay's ultimate food area. Gastropub near the pier? Casual seafood by the ocean? You're spoiled for choice.

MANHATTAN   BEACH

3

BIKE

PATH

*Santa Monica
Bay*

ARTESIA

HERMOSA
BEACH

PACIFIC

Park up at
HERMOSA BEACH

Stop at Hermosa Beach for a refreshment and feel the punk history course through you: bands like Black Flag and Circle Jerks got their start at the bars here.

4

COAST

WEST   190T

HIGHWAY

South Bay *beaches are key to the U.S. surf scene – like Manhattan and Redondo, both name-checked in the Beach Boys'* "Surfin' U.S.A."

Kick back at
REDONDO BEACH PIER

5

Cruise along the International Boardwalk to the pier before chilling out with a craft beer. You've earned it.

| 0 kilometers | 1 |
| 0 miles | 1 |

REDONDO
BEACH

An afternoon cycling along
the Strand

Sandy beaches, swaying palm trees, and a refreshing ocean breeze: L.A.'s coastline really does make for an idyllic cycle. And, thanks to a paved path known as the Strand, cyclists have 22 miles (35 km) of picturesque beachfront to pedal along. Our tip? Forget the stretch of the Strand that snakes alongside Santa Monica and Venice beaches, which are often overrun with tourists. Instead, start at Manhattan Beach, where a 5-mile (8-km) section is much less crowded and perfectly encapsulates L.A.'s coastal culture. And, yes, a postpedal drink is a must.

**1. Manhattan Beach
E-Bike Rentals**
3616 Highland Avenue,
Manhattan Beach;
www.mbebike.com
///going.deals.pardon

2. Bruce's Beach
2600 Highland Avenue,
Manhattan Beach
///wakes.normal.amuse

3. Manhattan Beach Pier
2 Manhattan Beach
Boulevard
///clash.deeply.copies

4. Hermosa Beach
1 Pier Avenue
///hooked.prove.bikes

5. Redondo Beach Pier
Fisherman's Wharf,
Redondo Beach
///achieving.oils.spin

With a little research and preparation, this city will feel like a home away from home. Check out these websites to ensure a healthy, safe stay in Los Angeles.

Los Angeles
DIRECTORY

SAFE SPACES

Los Angeles is a wonderfully diverse and largely progressive city, but should you feel uneasy or want to find your community at any point, there are spaces and resources to help you out.

www.discoverlosangeles.com/visit/the-guide-to-black-owned-businesses-in-la#chapter-overview
Find Black-owned businesses across L.A.

www.elawc.org
Center offering social and advocacy services for women, with an emphasis on Latinx communities.

www.lacatholics.org/interreligious-resources
A list of local, national, and global interfaith resources compiled by L.A. Catholics.

www.lalgbtcenter.org
Nonprofit organization running events and offering support for L.A.'s huge LGBTQ+ community.

HEALTH

Health care in the U.S. isn't free, so it's important to take out comprehensive health insurance for your visit. If you do need medical assistance, there are many pharmacies and hospitals across Los Angeles.

https://coronavirus.lacity.org/testing-center-map
A map of COVID-19 testing sites.

www.cvs.com/store-locator/cvs-pharmacy-locations/24-hour-pharmacies/California/Los-Angeles
Store locator showing 24-hour CVS pharmacies in the city.

www.dhs.lacounty.gov/find-a-clinic-or-hospital
The official website for L.A. county's Department of Health Services lists the area's hospitals and health centers.

www.outofthecloset.org/testing
This thrift store chain, which supports the AIDS Healthcare Foundation, runs a free HIV testing program.

www.plannedparenthood.org
National nonprofit organization providing sexual health care for all.

TRAVEL SAFETY INFORMATION
Before you travel – and while you're here – check the latest advice on how to stay safe in L.A. and the U.S.

www.flylax.com/travelsafely
Los Angeles International Airport's official travel safety guide.

www.lapdonline.org/crime-prevention
Safety tips and information on how to report various crimes.

www.lapublichealth.org
The L.A. County Department of Public Health advises on disease prevention.

www.parks.ca.gov
Official site for California's state parks, with information on safety.

www.travel.state.gov
Latest travel safety information from the U.S. government.

ACCESSIBILITY
L.A. is often hailed as one of the best cities in the U.S. when it comes to accessibility. Most public transportation, hotels, and attractions are available to all people, but it's always best to check ahead.

www.acb.org
National organization providing resources and support to blind and partially sighted people.

www.brailleinstitute.org/losangeles
The Braille Institute Los Angeles' center runs workshops, seminars, and events.

www.dcrc.co
Designed and operated by people with disabilities, the Disability Community Resource Center provides resources, training, and support for the community.

https://disability.lacity.org
The official website for the City of Los Angeles' Department on Disability.

INDEX

ABOUT THE ILLUSTRATOR

Mantas Tumosa

Creative designer and illustrator Mantas moved from his home country of Lithuania to London back in 2011. By day, he's busy creating bold, minimalistic illustrations that tell a story – such as the gorgeous cover of this book. By night, he's dreaming of adventures away, catching up on the basketball and cooking Italian food (which he can't get enough of).

Main Contributors Sarah Bennett, Ryan Gajewski, Anita Little, Eva Recinos

Senior Editor Lucy Richards

Senior Designers Tania Gomes, Ben Hinks

Project Editor Elspeth Beidas

Editors Rebecca Flynn, Zoë Rutland

US Editor Jennette ElNaggar

Project Art Editor Bharti Karakoti

Designer Jordan Lambley

Proofreader Stephanie Smith

Senior Cartographic Editor Casper Morris

Cartography Manager Suresh Kumar

Cartographer Ashif

Jacket Designer Tania Gomes, Jordan Lambley

Jacket Illustrator Mantas Tumosa

Senior Production Editor Jason Little

Production Controller Samantha Cross

Managing Editor Hollie Teague

Managing Art Editor Sarah Snelling

Art Director Maxine Pedliham

Publishing Director Georgina Dee

First edition 2022

Published in Great Britain by Dorling Kindersley Limited, DK, One Embassy Gardens, 8 Viaduct Gardens, London SW11 7BW, UK

The authorised representative in the EEA is Dorling Kindersley Verlag GmbH. Arnulfstr. 124, 80636 Munich, Germany

Published in the United States by DK Publishing, 1745 Broadway, 20th Floor, New York, NY 10019, USA

Copyright © 2022 Dorling Kindersley Limited
A Penguin Random House Company
22 23 24 25 10 9 8 7 6 5 4 3 2 1

All rights reserved.

The publishers cannot accept responsibility for any consequences arising from the use of this book, nor for any material on third party websites, and cannot guarantee that any website address in this book will be a suitable source of travel information.

A CIP catalog record for this book is available from the British Library.

A catalog record for this book is available from the Library of Congress.

ISSN: 1542 1554
ISBN: 9780 2415 6851 4

Printed and bound in China.

www.dk.com

MIX
Paper from responsible sources
FSC
www.fsc.org   **FSC™ C018179**

This book was made with Forest Stewardship Council™ certified paper – one small step in DK's commitment to a sustainable future. For more information go to www.dk.com/our-green-pledge

A NOTE FROM DK EYEWITNESS

The world is fast-changing and it's keeping us folk at DK Eyewitness on our toes. We've worked hard to ensure that this edition of Los Angeles Like a Local is up-to-date and reflects today's favourite places but we know that standards shift, venues close and new ones pop up in their place. So, if you notice something has closed, we've got something wrong or left something out, we want to hear about it. Drop us a line at travelguides@dk.com